Praise for *American C*

"There are few issues in American life where the stakes are as high as gun violence, nor where the steps to prevent it are more straightforward. Virtually every American wants to see changes put in place to strengthen our laws and enforcement mechanisms to make gun violence more rare. Yet, those changes have been much harder to enact than popular sentiment would dictate. Why is that? Tom Gabor and Fred Guttenberg lay out why in this exceptional book, which explains the lies, half-truths, and myths propagated by the gun industry to fight common sense gun laws and to sell as many guns as possible, no matter the lives lost or cost to our society. For those of us in the gun violence prevention movement— which is all Americans wanting a safer country where gun violence is rare—this book provides all you need to break through those lies and mistruths, and help lead and participate in conversations that can result in real change, where public safety laws are advanced that protect all Americans from gun violence.

—Kris Brown, president of Brady, United Against Gun Violence

"Let me say at the outset that Fred Guttenberg and I agree on very little when it comes to gun policy. But we listen to each other, and we constantly search for common ground. This book written by Thomas Gabor and Fred Guttenberg is an important one. And even though I disagree with some of what's written here, I recommend this book to anyone interested in saving lives. Fred and Tom make a passionate & evidenced-based case for facts to consider when pursuing certain reforms, which I'm sure will spur further passionate debate on this issue between us. I highly recommend *American Carnage*."

—Former Congressman Joe Walsh of Illinois's 8th district

"*American Carnage* by authors Thomas Gabor and Fred Guttenberg is a must read. Fred, like far too many Americans, understands gun violence because of the murder of his daughter Jaime. His work with Thomas Gabor to take on the myths around guns and gun violence in America and to present an evidence-based approach has resulted in a book that should be read by everyone who cares about this issue."

—Congressman Eric Swalwell, US Representative to California's 15th congressional district

"What a powerful book! *American Carnage* is an essential read for anyone seeking to counter fiction with fact in their efforts to reduce gun violence in the United States."

—Cassandra Crifasi, co-director of the Center for Gun Violence Solutions, The Bloomberg School of Public Health, Johns Hopkins University

"Organized around the prolific myths surrounding the gun debate—and there are a great many—the authors, a criminologist and an activist, are motivated by a simple principle: that facts matter. In service to that principle, Gabor and Guttenberg's highly readable and engaging book is a valuable contribution to truth in the otherwise often murky story of America and its guns."

—Robert J. Spitzer, professor emeritus at SUNY Cortland and author of *The Gun Dilemma* and *The Politics of Gun Control*

"This book, one I will go back to many times, gives you every essential tool to become a well-informed member of a club I want you to join: committed citizens lifting their voices for the lifesaving changes to gun laws the vast majority of Americans want."

—Steve Kerr, son, husband, father, grandfather, and head coach of the Golden State Warriors

"There's no single voice more important in the conversation in America about gun safety and avoiding the unthinkable tragedy of losing a child to gun violence than Fred Guttenberg. Fred's voice rings like a clarion in *American Carnage* where he, along with Thomas Gabor, explores the crucially important issue of misinformation when it comes to gun violence. The assault on truth spreads through every aspect of American politics, and there is no issue more uniquely American or deadly than gun violence. *American Carnage* is an essential read on one of the most important issues of our time."

—Nicolle Wallace, host of *Deadline: White House* on MSNBC and former White House communications director

"This vital, accessible book offers a clear-eyed, deeply researched response to the flood of disinformation about guns and gun-related violence. Required reading for all who wish to stem the surging tide of gun carnage."

—Caroline Light, director of the undergraduate women, gender, and sexuality studies program at Harvard University

"*American Carnage* is a must-read for every gun violence prevention advocate and those interested in the complexities of the gun violence issue in America. Skillfully written and engaging, *American Carnage* lays bare the falsehoods and myths that have been circulated over decades by those most willing to profit from their acceptance and proliferation. This book is a fact-filled roadmap for 'debunking' the disinformation which has made gun violence prevention such a complicated issue."

—Donna Wald, president of Grandmothers Against Gun Violence MA

"Smart, concise, well-written, and, perhaps more importantly, well-researched with non-biased, well-respected resource organizations. In debunking the many myths prevalent in the contemporary gun debates, the authors prove with facts and logic, glib slogans do not an argument make. The definitive resource on the misconceptions surrounding our gun culture debates. Highly recommended especially for advocates on both sides of the debate and the general public."

—Patricia Hatch, founding member and former president of Cape Cod Grandmothers Against Gun Violence

"Since 2020, gun violence has become the leading cause of death for American children. That fact alone should make everyone who cares about a child read this book. We buckle our children into car seats, install pool fences, teach them not to take drugs or go with strangers. We give them medicine when they are sick and protect them from dangerous situations. It is long overdue that we protect them from the most dangerous threat of all—gun violence.

"This book is clearly written and easy to read. It is packed with well-researched, evidence-based facts. The myth-busting in this book provides new information even to long-time supporters of firearm regulation. This is the information that makes us better advocates for the kind of sensible gun laws that will save our children."

—Susan Foley, MD, and Rebecca Cohen, co-leaders of Speaking Up for America/Indivisible

"In *American Carnage*, Thomas Gabor and Fred Guttenberg masterfully tackle many of the common myths and misperceptions about firearms and gun violence in America. They provide an even-handed approach to sharing evidence-based facts and the realities of this complex issue in a way that will be approachable to audiences. In short, *American Carnage* is a strong primer for anyone looking to inform themselves about the bevy of issues surrounding the issue of firearms in the US."

—Jaclyn Schildkraut, PhD, executive director of the Regional Gun Violence Research Consortium, Rockefeller Institute of Government, and national expert on mass shootings

"A serious and frank discussion on how to reduce firearm injuries and deaths must begin with truth. Tom Gabor and Fred Guttenberg undertake the Herculean task of exposing 'alternative facts' in the gun debate for what they really are: half-truths, myths, and, in some instances, outright lies. *American Carnage* is a seminal work because it lays the groundwork for an open and honest national dialogue on one of the most pressing problems of our time: gun violence."

—Louis Klarevas, research professor at Teachers College, Columbia University, and author of *Rampage Nation: Securing America from Mass Shootings*

AMERICAN CARNAGE

Books by the Authors

Thomas Gabor

The Prediction of Criminal Behaviour: Statistical Approaches (1986)
Armed Robbery: Cops, Robbers, and Victims (1987)
Everybody Does It: Crime by the Public (1994)
Basics of Criminology (2010)
Confronting Gun Violence in America (2016)
ENOUGH: Solving America's Gun Violence Crisis (2019)
CARNAGE: Preventing Mass Shootings in America (2021)

Fred Guttenberg

Find the Helpers: What 9/11 and Parkland Taught Me About Recovery, Purpose, and Hope (2020)

AMERICAN CARNAGE

Shattering the Myths
That Fuel Gun Violence

THOMAS GABOR
FRED GUTTENBERG

mango
PUBLISHING

CORAL GABLES

Cover Design and Layout: Roberto Núñez

For permission requests, please contact the publisher at:
Mango Publishing Group
2850 S Douglas Road, 2nd Floor
Coral Gables, FL 33134 USA
info@mango.bz

For special orders, quantity sales, course adoptions and corporate sales, please email the publisher at sales@mango.bz. For trade and wholesale sales, please contact Ingram Publisher Services at customer.service@ingramcontent.com or +1.800.509.4887.

American Carnage: Shattering the Myths That Fuel Gun Violence

Library of Congress Cataloging-in-Publication number: 2022952086
ISBN: (paperback) 978-1-68481-205-9, (hard cover) 978-1-68481-281-3,
      (ebook) 978-1-68481-206-6
BISAC category code: SOC051000, SOCIAL SCIENCE / Violence in Society

Printed in the United States of America

Dedication

This book is dedicated to something very precious and endangered today: the pursuit of truth. The open-minded pursuit of the truth is the foundation of democracy and human advancement. Lies and misinformation only serve bullies who hope to confuse and dupe others so their version of reality can prevail. Misinformation on gun violence serves only those who are profiting from the sale of guns or those wishing to justify maintaining a personal arsenal of weapons. With so many divergent narratives circulating in both mainstream and social media, it is vital to keep shedding light on the truth.

Truth matters because we cannot talk to one another, much less conduct a serious debate, until we share some principles and facts about the world at large.

This book is also dedicated to all survivors of gun violence who understand in the most painful, deep, and personal ways the impact that the failure of truth has had on society and its relationship to guns. We further dedicate this book to the fighters for democracy who understand that guns and threats to democracy are connected.

Table of Contents

FOREWORD

Fred Guttenberg and I are both members of a club that we never wanted to be a part of—one that nobody ever signs up for, but hundreds of Americans join every day. It's the "club" of the millions of survivors who have lost loved ones to the horrors of gun violence. We want to slam the doors to the club shut, and keep our friends, families, and all whom we love from joining, but we need your help. We need your voice.

I lost my father to gun violence in 1984. I was a freshman in college—barely eighteen—and my family's lives were shattered. Our sense of safety and innocence was gone in a flash, and we have lived with the pain of our loss every day since then. At the time of my dad's murder, I hadn't given a lot of thought to gun violence. I was a kid enjoying life, somewhat oblivious to the issue. I would read stories about shootings and, while it affected me emotionally, I couldn't feel the pain that the survivors of gun violence were experiencing. Everything changed after my dad died. With each gun-related death I read about, I'd agonize over the victims' families' pain, knowing exactly the despair they were feeling. As America's gun violence worsened, with mass shootings becoming routine, I felt more and more outraged. How could this be happening in our country? Why weren't we doing anything about it? Why wasn't our government doing anything about it?

I knew I wanted to be part of a solution, or at least part of a movement, but I didn't really know what that meant. I wanted to speak up, to say *something*, but it took me a long time to find my voice. Finally in 2016, something clicked for me. As I stood on the floor for the national anthem before Game 5 of the NBA Finals, the PA announcer asked the crowd to join a moment of silence for the forty-nine Pulse nightclub victims who had been brutally murdered the day before. This was the fifth moment of silence for mass shooting victims we had observed since the season began, and I was demoralized. These ceremonies were the right thing to do, but they felt so futile. Gun violence was out of control. Our government was failing to protect its citizens. Over a hundred people a day were dying in America from gun violence and all we could offer was moments of silence? Thoughts and prayers? Rather than addressing the issue head-on with ideas and solutions to save lives, our government did nothing, paralyzed by the extreme partisanship that has defined modern American life. It was disgusting. And so I decided to say something. I went on a podcast and called out our government for its lack of action. Because I was the coach of the Warriors—a hugely popular team with a worldwide following—my comments made it into the media. People took notice. I got plenty of support and lots of backlash. I started hearing from leaders of different gun violence prevention groups around the country. I began to take part in fundraising efforts for groups like Brady, Giffords, and Sandy Hook Promise. I met other survivors. And through all these new relationships, I really started to learn about gun violence, about the politics involved, about how important words and phrases are when discussing the issue, about strategies for speaking with someone who might have opposing views, and about how we can actually create change. I was now officially part of the movement.

Tragically, it was not many months later that Fred Guttenberg joined "the club." I'll never forget the day of the Parkland school shooting: Valentine's Day, 2018. I was sitting in a Portland hotel room getting ready for a game that night, when the news came of the horrific shooting that took seventeen lives and left so many more shattered. I turned on the TV, wanting to know what was happening, crying at the scenes, and knowing what so many families were about to feel when they heard the unimaginable news, just like I did in 1984. Their lives would never be the same. Over the ensuing months, I watched as so many survivors stood up and courageously expressed their loss, anger, and pain. From the Parkland students who formed March For Our Lives to parents like Manuel Oliver and Fred Guttenberg who powerfully stood up to the gun lobby and called out those responsible for our country's inaction, I watched as "the club" grew. It was excruciating yet inspiring, hopeless yet also hopeful. I knew that more mass shootings would follow, that more innocent people would lose their lives, and that more survivors would suffer. But seeing Fred's courage in the face of such devastating loss gave me hope.

In *Find the Helpers*, Fred's book about becoming a leading voice in gun violence prevention in the wake of losing his beautiful and ebullient daughter Jaime, he shares that his main identity is that of a dad. Dad to his son Jesse, and still and always Dad to his Jaime. It is **this** identity that fuels and spurs his activism, even while carrying his grief every day—like myself and every other survivor. Fred's powerful voice and his ability to educate the world and change our laws would not have been possible without Fred finding *his* helpers. Countless individuals across the country—activists and civic leaders, homemakers and students, politicians, pundits, artists, and change-makers—have also lifted their voices and lifted Fred in the movement to make real change.

In *American Carnage*, Fred joins renowned author Tom Gabor to give us the natural follow-up to *Find the Helpers*, as well as Tom's books *Carnage* and *Enough*, by laying out some of the most dangerous and distorted lies manufactured by the gun industry. The industry has used these lies to stop us from taking action collectively. By breaking down these lies with a barrage of truth, facts, and data, as has been so capably done in *American Carnage*, the hope is that we can finally have the factual conversations necessary to end gun violence in our country. For too many of us, the issue of firearms and the pointed accusations and rhetoric that swirl around it feels too "political." But in order to save lives—potentially those of your own loved ones—discussing these issues with your friends and family is a crucial step toward creating real change. And learning about the issues will make those discussions much more productive.

So, where can you start? It's simple. Read this book. Fred and I, as survivors, as parents, and as Americans who want this country to live up to its promise, ask that you spend some time educating yourself about why the regulation of firearms matters. Question efforts that rewrite our history of strong regulation by those seeking to make a profit at any cost, and consider how *you* can talk about the change needed to save lives in a thoughtful, direct, and impactful manner that connects with anyone, whether they own guns or not. This book will give you the tools and confidence to go forward and be the best advocate for yourself, your family, and your community that you can be.

It is my belief that America can and will create the changes necessary to our gun laws to save the lives of its citizens. Ninety percent of Americans, regardless of political leanings, support universal background checks. Seventy percent of NRA members believe in them. The majority of us also believe that no citizen should own assault rifles or have access to high-capacity magazines—the weapons and ammunition involved in most mass shootings. The problem is not sensibility. The vast majority of people in this country are rational and sensible. The problem is politics. But, like every other major issue this country has dealt with in our history, political change takes time, like turning a cruise ship. In 2008, Barack Obama, a progressive democrat, ran for president on a platform that did not support gay marriage. The issue was considered politically dangerous, so Obama shied away from it. But public opinion changed and, just seven years later in 2015, while Obama was still president, gay marriage became legal. Now gay marriage is widely accepted by Americans and is no longer a political issue. Yes, gun violence is a different, more heated, and contested issue, but the politics are similar. As public sentiment changes, our laws can reflect that. Gun owners and non gun owners across America are disgusted with gun violence. We can and will enact the necessary changes to our gun laws when public opinion becomes so strong that the pendulum swings and politicians are forced to act. In fact this is already happening. In 2022, ten Republican senators actually signed a bill, albeit a modest one, expanding background checks on people under twenty-one and encouraging states to enact "red flag" laws on potential gun buyers. It was the first bipartisan bill of its kind in several decades. Yes, more is needed, but the tide is shifting.

The bottom line is that we need as many people on board this train as possible. As a coach, I know the power of collaboration. Our motto with the Warriors is "Strength in Numbers." The more people who are aligned and dedicated to a cause, the more likely it is for that cause to come to life. It's true in basketball and true in life. We rise or fall on the strength of our collective capability and each person doing his or her part. Our democracy is no different. This book, one I will go back to many times, gives you every essential tool to become a well-informed member of a club I *want* you to join: committed citizens lifting their voices for the lifesaving changes to gun laws the vast majority of Americans want.

So, please read this book and then make a difference with the facts and knowledge you gain. We need you on this team. A team whose legacy is the lives we will save together.

—Steve Kerr, son, husband, father, grandfather, and head coach of the
Golden State Warriors

Chapter 1

COMBATTING MISINFORMATION ON GUN VIOLENCE

United States Senator Hiram Johnson once said that the first casualty of war was the truth.[1] The debate over guns and gun violence is nothing short of a clash of cultures over how to best achieve personal security. And truth has been a major casualty of this clash. Outrageous claims are often made about such things as the meaning of the Second Amendment to the US Constitution, the value of gun ownership as a self-defense tool, the protection certain gun laws may provide, and even the number of guns and gun owners in America.

One reason for the many false claims in this area is that gun violence research has been starved of funds, leaving a huge void in our understanding of many issues, including basic ones such as the number of guns and gun owners in the country. For over twenty years, Congress kept the Centers for Disease Control and Prevention (CDC) from funding research on firearms through the Dickey Amendment, which threatened the CDC's funding.[2] This provision prohibits the use of federal funds to advocate or promote gun control. The amendment, introduced by Congressional Republicans, followed lobbying by the National Rifle

Association, which was becoming increasingly concerned about research that was showing that guns in the home increased the risk of a homicide. Sepsis, a potentially life-threatening condition caused by the body's response to an infection, kills the same number of people each year as gunfire, but receives 100 times the funding.[3]

There has also been a rejection of science by a segment of the population that ignores or minimizes the gun violence problem in the US, just as some Americans have refused to acknowledge the harm produced by the COVID-19 pandemic. Alex Jones, a far-right broadcaster, has even peddled the falsehood that major mass shootings, such as that at Sandy Hook Elementary School in Newtown, Connecticut, did not happen.[4] Jones has a large number of followers whom he has convinced that such events have been staged in order to serve as a pretext for tighter gun laws. A general distrust of government or cynicism in relation to broadening its powers predisposes some Americans to question any issue that might justify government expansion. The gun debate is so intense and acrimonious because it lies at the center of the great cultural divide in this country—a chasm that pits urbanites against rural dwellers and splits the country along racial, geographic, and educational lines.

Those rejecting research exposing the dangers associated with gun ownership tend to take the view that the "right to keep and bear arms" is an unlimited constitutional right. Therefore, for them, the science is moot. They believe they have an absolute right to acquire virtually any type of gun—case closed. As seen in Chapter 7, the interpretation of the Second Amendment of the US Constitution by the courts has evolved and is more nuanced than the simplistic notion that this right is unlimited. In fact, the "right to keep and bear arms" throughout most of this country's history was not recognized by the courts as an individual right at all, but rather as a right to form a state militia. The right to firearms is different from, say, the freedom of speech, as an overly expansive view of gun rights can threaten the lives of others. For example, if it is permissible to carry an AR-15 rifle to a rally, this action may not only stifle the free speech of those who are intimidated but may threaten the lives of others present if an altercation breaks out.

A more recent line of argument asserts the right of the public to be protected from violence. Some legal scholars are arguing that the first duty of government is to protect citizens from abuses by public officials and from private actors.[5] The human rights group Amnesty International has condemned the US for failing to protect its citizens from gun violence by not developing a comprehensive system of firearm regulations. In a 2018 report, Amnesty writes, "The USA has failed to implement a comprehensive, uniform, and coordinated system of gun safety laws and regulations, particularly in light of the large number of firearms in circulation, which perpetuates unrelenting and potentially avoidable violence, leaving individuals susceptible to injury and death from firearms."[6]

The debate about the true costs/benefits of guns is one that is not just academic, nor only one waged by ordinary citizens in person or on social media. Egregious statements and claims are often made at hearings in Washington or state legislatures and used to prevent reform that can protect Americans. Recently, a federal judge overturned the thirty-year assault weapons ban in California, saying: "Like the Swiss Army Knife, the popular AR-15 rifle is a perfect combination of home-defense weapon and homeland defense equipment."[7] The judge failed to acknowledge the role of such military-style rifles in many of the deadliest mass shootings as well as in the murders of police officers. We are not aware of any mass killings with Swiss Army knives.

The NRA's Contributions to the Assault on Truth

While the National Rifle Association has been weakened by scandal, it has been a potent force in shaping policy on guns. Over the years, the organization morphed from one concerned about marksmanship and gun safety to a powerful lobby group that has opposed virtually any restrictions on guns or measures that could assess a buyer's suitability for gun ownership. As an illustration of the NRA's past, consider this statement to Congress by Karl Frederick, a president of the organization in the 1930s: "I do not believe in the general promiscuous toting of guns." By contrast, in the 1980s, the NRA was promoting "shall issue" laws that would make the carrying of weapons a virtual entitlement in most states.

The NRA has become an extremist organization, adopting an insurrectionist ideology hostile to government. Members of its board of directors have occasionally displayed the most vile, racist views. Ted Nugent, a former rock star and longstanding NRA board member, has made numerous racist statements. On one occasion, he said of South Africans: "All men are not created equal...The preponderance of South Africa is a different breed of man...They still put bones in their noses, they still walk around naked, they wipe their butts with their hands... These are different people. You give 'em toothpaste, they f---ing eat it...I hope they don't become civilized."[8]

As extreme as some of its officers' views are, the impact of the NRA's messaging on public opinion must be recognized if the views promoted by the organization are to be successfully challenged. While a smaller proportion of households owns guns than was the case a few decades ago, the public has become increasingly receptive to a gun rights message and there is a wider belief among the public that gun ownership and carrying guns can significantly improve the ability of people to protect themselves.

Polls have shown a growth in the percentage of Americans who believe a gun kept in the home makes them safer.

Surveys by Gallup conducted between 2000 and 2014 show that on the question of whether gun ownership makes a home safer or more dangerous, the public has reversed itself. In September 2000, 35 percent believed that a gun made a home safer, but, by October 2014, 63 percent held that view.[9] Thus, a majority have come to believe that guns enhance the safety of a home.[10] In 1959, a Gallup poll found that 60 percent of Americans favored banning handguns. That number dropped to 41 percent by 1975 and 24 percent in 2012. This change can be understood by examining the public's evolving understanding of the Second Amendment. By early 2008, according to Gallup, 73 percent of Americans believed the Second Amendment "guaranteed the rights of Americans to own guns" outside a militia.[11]

The gun lobby's impact on public opinion has also been seen in relation to the sharp decline in the public's support for a ban on assault weapons. A *Washington Post* poll conducted on December 13, 2015, showed this support at 45 percent, a drop from 80 percent revealed by the same poll taken in June 1994.[12] There has been some reversal of this drop accompanying the large number of mass shootings in recent years, but support has not so far come close to the levels of the mid-1990s.[13]

Another example of a shift in public opinion relates to the question of whether the priority in establishing gun policies should be to control gun ownership or to protect gun rights. The Pew Research Center has been asking this question since December 1993. At that time, just 34 percent of Americans said that gun rights should be a priority. In December 2014, for the first time, more Americans (52 percent) prioritized the protection of gun rights over controlling gun ownership.[14] Since then, most Pew polls show that the American public is now quite evenly divided on this question.

Public opinion polls reveal that Americans are becoming more afraid of mass shootings and terrorism.[15] Many of America's most deadly mass shootings have occurred since 2007. Other indications are that a larger proportion of gun owners are buying guns for self-protection and the number with carry permits has grown. It seems that the shift in public opinion reflects the gun lobby's success in convincing more Americans that arming oneself is the best form of protection. The NRA's former head, Wayne LaPierre, made precisely this pitch following the slaughter of children at Sandy Hook Elementary School in Newtown, Connecticut, when he declared, "The only thing that stops a bad guy with a gun is a good guy with a gun." Needless to say, this is both incorrect and a highly cynical view, as he implied that arming ordinary people is the only recourse our society has left in tackling gun violence.

Other familiar slogans coming from gun rights advocates include: "Guns don't kill people, people kill people," "When guns are outlawed, only outlaws have guns," and "An armed society is a polite society." These and other clever slogans make intuitive sense, but they collapse when scientific evidence is used to examine them. Slogans also misrepresent the positions of gun violence prevention advocates. The slogan beginning, "When guns are outlawed…" suggests that proponents of reasonable gun laws favor banning guns. Most Americans are not in favor of disarming the public, although they may support banning especially dangerous firearms, such as assault-type weapons. We are not aware of any credible organization or activist proposing the total disarmament of Americans.

Gun groups and the industry have invested a great deal of money on advertising intended to change public opinion. Much of their focus has been on stoking fear and convincing people that their right to own and carry arms is both threatened and unlimited. Little attention is devoted to the need to balance the rights of gun owners with the rights and interests of the public to be safe. Some gun owners believe that virtually any form of gun regulation is a violation of their constitutional rights. The true meaning of the Second Amendment to the Constitution is discussed in Chapter 7.

The aggressive promotion of armed self-defense that began in the 1980s was a response by the gun industry and lobby groups to declining sales stemming from a decline in shooting sports, urbanization, and the changing composition of the US population. These groups have been selling the need for self-protection from crime, social unrest, and government tyranny.[16] This is a very dangerous turn for gun groups, one that is fueling divisions in our society. The use of fear tactics to sell firearms is radicalizing gun rights supporters and leading to a narrative that guns are the only thing standing in the way of tyranny or a takeover by groups hostile to the "American" way of life. For the NRA, this narrative has been a radical departure from their beginnings as an organization aiming to improve marksmanship in the military. The polls show that the organization has been quite successful in selling this narrative.

Why We Wrote This Book

The aim of this book is to take on the assault on truth that has recently been waged in so many policy areas, including that of gun violence. The gun lobby, militant gun owners, and some researchers opposing gun regulations have spread misinformation about such things as the number of defensive gun uses and the effectiveness with which the average gun owner can use a firearm for self-defense or defense of property. Exaggerating the frequency of successful defensive gun uses supports gun sales and the narrative that an armed society is a safer society.

A public that is better informed will be less vulnerable to accepting such false narratives and will be more credible in pressuring lawmakers to pass more effective policies to stem the tide of gun violence. This book is also intended to inform the millions of activists who are on the front lines of this struggle. These activists are very passionate about this issue, as many have lost family members and/or friends to gun violence. We are in awe of their passion and wish to enhance their knowledge of guns and of the research in this area. Such knowledge is critical in elevating the credibility of the gun violence prevention movement, countering the arguments of the gun lobby, dealing with the press, effectively lobbying legislators, and promoting effective solutions to gun violence.

Strong evidence-based arguments, when repeated by activists throughout the country, can be effective in countering the many slogans and false statements repeated incessantly by spokespersons for the gun lobby and its surrogates. The gun lobby and some gun owners are so passionate about guns or so beholden to the gun industry that they have an interest in muddying the waters and distorting the truth.

One form of distortion is the notion that we have to choose between respecting the rights of gun owners to possess firearms and gun regulations that can promote public safety and save lives. This is a false choice and leads to the argument by gun rights advocates that any gun law is a violation of their constitutional rights or a prelude to the confiscation of all firearms. This is patent nonsense. One can keep a gun in the home without allowing children and teenagers to gain access to it. One can also own a gun that is equipped with features that can prevent deadly accidents, such as magazine safeties and loaded chamber indicators. We can carefully screen prospective gun owners for instability and a history of violence while continuing to recognize the right of stable, nonviolent people to own guns. Activists must show that this polarized thinking, the idea that you can only have either gun rights or gun regulation, is false and merely serves to paralyze our ability to deal with gun violence. This plays right into the hands of those who wish to do nothing about the violence.

Many of the beliefs challenged in this book have been promoted by gun lobbyists and groups who continue to push for increasingly permissive (weak) gun laws. For example, an increasing number of states (twenty-four, at last count) do not require a permit or training to carry a firearm. In addition, in June 2022, the US Supreme Court struck down a New York state law requiring that those carrying guns must show "proper cause" for so doing (e.g., business owners who carry large amounts of cash to the bank).[17] This ruling may be followed by similar challenges in the few remaining states in which a reason must be shown by those wishing to carry concealed firearms. In America, carrying a gun is effectively being recognized by an increasing number of states and by the nation's highest court as a constitutional right.

In the context of an enormous surge in gun violence and mass shootings in 2020 and 2021, the reader may be justified in asking: What about the right of the public at large to be safe? Do only gun owners and their rights matter? Don't federal and state governments have an obligation to protect us from violence? We will tackle some of these questions in the last chapter since the first author, as well as legal scholars, has made the case that the Declaration of Independence, the Constitution, and international agreements signed or ratified by the US obligate our lawmakers to protect us from gun violence.

Organization of the Book

The chapters that follow cover different topics on guns and gun violence (e.g., guns in US history, guns and self-defense, and so on). Each chapter presents a number of myths that are then refuted by employing scientific evidence that has been published in scholarly publications and other respected published sources. Each chapter also contains a summary of the evidence presented. The final chapter discusses how misinformation on gun violence can be countered. Appendix A presents a *Declaration of the Right to Live Free from Gun Violence* drafted by Tom Gabor. Based on America's founding documents, this *Declaration* affirms the right of Americans to live, work, shop, attend school and public meetings, worship, and engage in leisure activities free of the constant threat of gun violence. The *Declaration* offers a counternarrative to those who hold the mistaken belief that the Second Amendment affords an unlimited right to possess and carry guns.

Chapter 2

THE TRUTH ABOUT GUNS IN US HISTORY AND CULTURE

Myth 1: Gun Laws Are a Recent Development

There is a general belief that little gun regulation existed throughout American history and that laws regulating guns are a recent development. Western movies were likely influential in creating the impression that the frontier was full of gun-toting men who were ready to draw their guns at the slightest provocation. This view of the US frontier paves the way for those advocating the expansion of gun rights to argue that laws allowing people to carry guns openly in public settings such as bars, colleges, and government buildings are only returning us to the norms that existed throughout American history.

Fact Check: The belief that gun laws did not exist in the early years of the republic, or that they were very lax, is patently false. Historians tell us, for example, that contrary to Hollywood depictions, the Old West had low rates of violence and many gun ordinances prohibited gun carrying in towns and inside bars.

Adam Winkler, a professor of constitutional law at the University of California in Los Angeles (UCLA), has written that gun regulation in frontier towns was quite strict. In notorious Dodge City, Kansas, for example, people were required to turn in their guns when they entered the town. Contrary to the mythology of violence-ridden Western towns beset by shootouts, an average of just one to two murders per year occurred in Dodge City during the cattle era.[18] Winkler also notes that the epic gunfight at the OK Corral in Tombstone, Arizona, occurred when lawman Wyatt Earp and his brothers tried to enforce a gun ordinance by disarming a semi-outlaw group called the Cowboys.

Ray Allen Billington, a historian specializing in the study of the American frontier and the West, notes that businesspeople and other leaders in Western cattle towns were quick to establish local police forces and to enforce prohibitions against carrying guns. Disarmament was routinely practiced in newly established Western towns and was generally understood as a means of improving public safety. According to Billington, the shootouts glorified in countless books and movies were "unheard of."[19]

Professor Winkler of UCLA adds that the Revolutionary Era was marked by strict gun laws by which all free men were mandated to acquire militarily useful firearms and to attend periodic gatherings (musters), during which the guns were inspected and recorded by officials—an early type of gun registration.[20] In some states (e.g., New Hampshire), officials conducted door-to-door inventories of guns available in the community, and the states could seize guns if they were needed for military purposes. Gun regulation was also prevalent in the South, a region with some of the most restrictive gun laws in the nineteenth century. These laws were designed to prevent gunfights and to disarm Black people following the Civil War. Laws banning the carrying of concealed weapons were widespread and generally believed to be an essential part of preventing violence.[21] Therefore, contrary to a prevalent belief, gun regulation is not a twentieth century phenomenon.

Political scientist Robert Spitzer notes:

> …[T]hough gun possession is as old as America, so too are gun laws. But there's more: gun laws were not only ubiquitous, numbering in the thousands, but also spanned every conceivable category of regulation, from gun acquisition, sale, possession, transport, and use, including deprivation of use through outright confiscation, to hunting and recreational regulations, to registration and express gun bans.[22]

As early as 1686, New Jersey prohibited wearing weapons because they were said to induce "great Fear and Quarrels." Alabama's 1839 law banning the carrying of concealed weapons was titled, "An Act to Suppress the Evil Practice of Carrying Weapons Secretly." Furthermore, by the early 1900s, over forty states outlawed or restricted gun carrying due to rising violence. Spitzer asks about the current trend toward more gun carrying: "Why must we relearn a lesson we codified centuries ago? How dumb are we?"[23]

Myth 2: An Increasing Percentage of Americans Are Buying Guns

There is a widespread belief that gun ownership levels in the US are continuing to climb. Many believe that a majority of Americans are gun owners. The National Shooting Sports Foundation stated the following in 2012: "Violent crime has fallen 65 percent since 1993. While there are many factors in the mix, it is incontrovertible that firearms ownership continued to grow, by astronomical rates, over the same time period."[24] The Foundation is not so subtly saying that the fall in violent crime is due at least in part to the growth in gun ownership. Therefore, according to the Foundation, guns protect us from crime.

Fact Check: While there are indications that gun ownership has risen somewhat during the pandemic, there is no evidence of an increase over the last few decades. Did gun ownership in fact grow from 1993 to 2012, as suggested by the National Shooting Sports Foundation? Nobody has a precise count of the number of guns in America or the proportion of citizens who are gun owners. In fact, it is a violation of federal law to use the national background check system to create a national database of guns owned by Americans.[25] Therefore, we rely on surveys of representative samples of the population. While the number of guns in America continues to grow, so does the total population, which is why it is important to examine the percentage of adults who own guns or to calculate, say, the number of guns per every 100 people.

The US is a clear outlier with regard to its arsenal of privately owned firearms, surpassing other nations by a wide margin both in terms of the absolute number of guns and in the number of guns relative to its population. The most credible recent estimate, taking into account guns that are no longer operational, is about 400 million total firearms in the US, or about 120 guns for every 100 people.[26] Recent polls show that 30 percent of American adults own a gun.[27]

While there have been some spikes in gun ownership over the last few decades, including a surge in gun purchases during the pandemic, the overall trend is clearly heading downward over the last 40 years at least. According to the National Opinion Research Center, household gun ownership declined from 50 percent in 1977 to 31 percent in 2014.[28]

Changing demographics, urbanization, the decline of hunting, and the lack of a military draft have all played a role in this decline.

The proportion of households involved in hunting is half of what it was in the mid-1970s.[29] The decline in hunting is in turn a result of declining rural populations and changes in social attitudes relating to hunting. Changing demographics and the end of conscription into military service in 1973 are other reasons given for the decline in household gun ownership. Specifically, the growing Hispanic and Asian populations have lower gun ownership levels than white Americans, and the lack of a draft means that fewer Americans are introduced to firearms through military service. One factor has become more relevant as a reason for purchasing guns: self-protection. The Pew Research Center has found that the proportion of those citing protection as the reason for buying a gun rose from 26 percent in 1999 to 48 percent in 2013.[30]

The surges in sales following certain shootings illustrate the importance of self-protection as a motive for gun purchases.[31] The mass shooting in an Aurora, Colorado, movie theater in the summer of 2012 was followed by a dramatic jump in firearms applications and enrollments in firearms classes. Similar increases in applications were observed following the shootings on the Virginia Tech campus in 2007 and the near assassination of Congresswoman Gabrielle Giffords of Arizona in 2011. The FBI has also documented spikes in background checks following high-profile mass shootings. Individuals purchasing guns exclusively for self-protection are not those with a gun fetish or obsession. They may even buy guns reluctantly, feeling that self-preservation is at stake.

The increasing frequency of purchases of guns for self-protection may lead people to believe that gun ownership overall is increasing. However, the forces described—declining rural populations and hunting, the changing demographic composition of the US population, and the end of the draft—have collectively led to a net decline in the number of households owning guns.

Myth 3: America Has an All-Encompassing Gun Culture

There is an impression globally that not only is the US awash in guns but that most Americans are gun owners, are fascinated by guns, and are part of a form of "gun culture." A British Broadcasting Corporation (BBC) report refers to "America's gun culture" and provides charts showing that the US is a global outlier when it comes to gun ownership and gun-related homicides.[32] The data presented are accurate, but do Americans as a whole embrace guns and permissive gun laws?

Fact Check: Currently, about four in ten US households own one or more guns and three in ten Americans personally own a firearm.[33] Therefore, gun owners and gun-owning households are in the minority.

The absence of a uniform American gun culture is also shown by the differences in gun ownership across regions and states. Just 16 percent of adults in the Northeast personally own a gun, whereas gun ownership is double this number in the other regions of the US.[34] The states range from Montana, where 64 percent of adults live in a household with one or more guns, to New Jersey and Hawaii, where just 8 percent of adults live in a household with a gun.[35]

A Pew Research Center survey shows that there are also wide gender, age, and ethnic/racial gaps in gun ownership.[36] Men are far more likely to personally own a gun than women (39 percent of men versus 22 percent of women). Whites are far more likely to own a gun than Black or Hispanic people (36 percent versus 24 percent and 15 percent, respectively). Rural residents are far more likely to personally own a gun than urban dwellers (46 percent versus 19 percent). White, rural males who are middle-aged or older are the most armed group in the American population. These figures indicate that many groups do not embrace a gun "culture."

Yet another indication that the American public as a whole does not have a gun fetish is a survey that probed the number of Americans carrying guns on a daily basis. The study found that nine million (about 3 percent of the population) carried a loaded handgun at least once a month and three million (1 percent of the population) carried on a daily basis.[37] So much for the idea that all Americans tote guns regularly and participate in a uniform, all-encompassing gun culture. Even these numbers may fail to tell the full story, since we must distinguish between those who carry guns as symbols of self-reliance, masculinity, and a way of life (usually in rural areas) and those who purchase and learn to use guns to prevent their own victimization. The latter group cannot be said to belong to any form of distinct culture. They merely wish to live and believe that gun ownership will allow them to do so.

Surveys also reveal that many Americans reject the weak gun laws in America and prioritize public safety over gun rights. For more than twenty-five years, the Pew Research Center has been asking Americans whether it was more important to prioritize gun rights or to control gun ownership.[38] On eleven occasions between 1993 and 2008, Pew found that majorities consistently said it was more important to control gun ownership than to protect the right of Americans to own guns. However, since 2009, public opinion has been more evenly divided. Then, following the Sandy Hook school shooting in Newtown, Connecticut, public opinion again tilted in favor of controlling gun ownership over protecting gun rights (49 percent vs. 42 percent). By May 2013, opinion was again divided as 50 percent said it was more important to control gun ownership, while 48 percent said it was more important to protect gun rights. Then, in December 2014, gun rights prevailed by six points over controlling gun ownership. However, in July 2015, Pew once again found that respondents prioritized gun restrictions over gun rights by a narrow margin (50 percent versus 47 percent). In June 2017, 52 percent of American adults favored stricter gun laws, 18 percent favored easing gun laws and 30 percent believed that the current laws are "just right."[39] More recently, following the high-fatality mass shootings in Buffalo, New York and Uvalde, Texas in May 2022, an ABC News/Ipsos Poll found that 70 percent of Americans prioritized enacting new gun laws, while just 29 prioritized the rights of gun owners.[40]

Recent surveys have begun to document an increasing concentration of guns in the possession of a smaller number of owners. While the total number of guns is not declining, the number of owners as a percentage of the population is going down. What we are seeing is gun ownership becoming concentrated in the hands of a smaller number of Americans who form a core group of firearm owners. A Harvard/Northeastern University study found that 20 percent of US gun owners (about 6 percent of US adults) own 65 percent of the guns in the country.[41]

While polls continue to show that the public remains divided on the issue of gun restrictions versus the rights of owners, surging violence and the increasing parade of high-casualty shootings seems to have shifted public opinion. It can be safely said that at least half of American adults do not embrace the view that gun ownership and associated rights should take precedence over public safety and the regulation of guns.

Myth 4: Most Americans Support an Expansive View of Gun Rights and Generally Oppose Restrictions on Gun Ownership

Fact Check: Most Americans are not gun owners, and surveys show that the majority of citizens, including most gun owners, support basic, sensible gun laws. While the public may be split with regard to issues such as the benefits of keeping a gun in the home, it is false to argue that our inability to enact smart and effective gun laws is due to our failure to agree on any measures. For example, polls over the last decade have shown that about eight to nine of every ten Americans, and even a majority of NRA members, support conducting criminal and related background checks on all gun buyers.[42] Currently, a significant proportion of gun sales occur on the private market (through the Internet and gun shows) and do not require background checks.

Following the mass shooting at Columbine High School in 1999, the NRA's CEO, Wayne LaPierre, declared the organization's support for instant background checks at gun shows, which accounted for many of the private sales at the time.[43] Unfortunately, that organization, which was initially formed to promote improved marksmanship for military personnel, has morphed into an extremist organization and adopted an insurrectionist ideology that is hostile to government and virtually any form of gun regulation. The organization has become increasingly beholden to the gun industry and is overseen by a board of directors, some of whom have expressed the most disrespectful and racist views.

From conversations following numerous speaking engagements, the first author learned that members of the public would be even more supportive of basic policies to prevent gun violence if they were better informed about laws and practices throughout America. For example, many people are surprised to hear that most Americans are not gun owners and are not a part of any form of "gun culture." They are struck by the fact that a small fraction of the population—superowners—possess many of the nation's guns.

Further illustrating the concern, rather than affinity, most Americans have in relation to gun ownership are surveys showing that large majorities would feel less rather than more safe if they learned that more people in their communities were carrying guns.[44] In addition, most citizens are opposed to gun carrying on college campuses, in government buildings, and in other sensitive areas. College and university administrators, faculty, students, and campus police chiefs are strongly unified in their opposition to guns on campus.[45] Majorities also support requiring a police permit to buy a gun, personalizing all new handguns so they can only be discharged by the lawful owners, preventing the mentally ill from buying guns, and banning assault weapons.[46] Thus, the majority of Americans favor many forms of restrictions on guns and gun ownership.

Guns in US History: The Bottom Line

- Gun laws are not a recent development in America. In fact, they were stricter during the Revolutionary Period and in frontier towns than they are in many states today. During the Revolutionary Period, states periodically took inventory of residents' guns and could seize them when firearms were needed for military service. Frontier towns were often quick to establish law enforcement and often banned the carrying of weapons in towns or saloons. The carrying of guns was prohibited in most states by the end of the 1800s. By contrast, all states today allow gun carrying and the majority either require no permit to do so or have laws that require them to issue a carry permit once an applicant meets some basic conditions (e.g., completing a gun safety course or passing a background check proving they have no felony criminal records on file).

- Household gun ownership in the US has been declining, not increasing, in the last few decades. Changing demographics, urbanization, the decline of hunting, and the lack of a draft have all played a role in this decline. While the number of guns continues to increase as the population grows, the proportion of gun owners as a percentage of the population is falling. The percentage of owners who purchase guns for self-protection rather than hunting has been increasing.

- Contrary to America's image, most Americans do not participate in a "gun culture." Seven in ten American adults do not own guns, and most of the nation's guns are owned by about 5 percent of the total population. There are significant regional, gender, age, and ethnic/racial differences in gun ownership. Rural residents are far more likely to own a gun than urban dwellers. Just 1 percent of Americans carry a gun on a daily basis. Far more Americans favor tightening, rather than easing, gun laws. At least half of

American adults do not embrace the view that gun ownership and associated rights should take precedence over public safety and the regulation of guns. Many new gun buyers are purchasing their weapons for self-protection rather than due to a fascination with guns. In addition, the large gaps in ownership among different demographic and residential groups illustrate that it is folly to speak about the US as a nation uniformly obsessed with guns.

- Most Americans do not believe in expanding gun rights and support a number of measures designed to prevent gun violence. A majority of Americans, including gun owners, support policies such as those requiring all gun buyers to go through a criminal background check. They have expressed concerns about the dangers of widespread gun carrying, feeling it would make them less, not more, safe. In addition, most citizens are opposed to gun carrying on college campuses, in government buildings, and in other sensitive areas. Majorities also support requiring a police permit to buy a gun, personalizing all new handguns so they can only be discharged by the lawful owners, preventing the mentally ill from buying guns, and banning assault weapons.

Chapter 3

THE TRUTH ABOUT GUNS AND PUBLIC SAFETY

Myth 5: An Armed Society Is a Polite Society

One of the favorite slogans of gun rights advocates is: "An armed society is a polite society." The idea here is that carrying weapons raises the level of civility in society by deterring individuals who may become violent from assaulting others. It is assumed that people will think twice before committing harm to others as armed individuals would always be present and could intervene.

Fact Check: If an armed society was indeed more polite, the US would be the safest and most polite among advanced societies. The US has the highest number of civilian-held guns per capita—120 guns for every 100 people, more than any other country.[47] We will leave it to others to determine the politeness of Americans relative to people in other countries. America does stand alone relative to other high-income countries with regard to its high levels of gun-related mortality.[48] In 2020, firearm-related injuries became the leading cause of death among American children and teens between one and nineteen years of age.[49] In addition, no other country comes close to experiencing the parade of mass shootings seen in the US—close to two per day in 2020 and 2021. No setting is immune, as Americans have seen mass shootings in schools and colleges, churches, airports, nightclubs, workplaces, movie theaters and shopping malls. Teenagers are often terrified to go to school. A seventeen-year-old senior at a north Philadelphia high school put it this way: "It's a hostile environment. It's a real war zone."[50]

Violence is widespread in the US, and most Americans have been touched by it either directly or indirectly. A survey of California residents found that nearly two out of three persons in the state have either experienced gun violence themselves, heard gunshots in their neighborhood at some point, encountered sidewalk memorials where violent deaths occurred, or knew someone who had either been shot or was at risk of a violent attack.[51] So much for an armed society being more polite.

Will more guns pacify the population? Evidence suggesting this premise is unlikely is found in some research showing that people who carry guns are more prone to aggressive behavior. A team of Harvard University researchers conducted a telephone survey of 790 licensed drivers in Arizona that examined the relationship between firearm carrying and hostile behavior on the roadway (a.k.a. "road rage").[52] Respondents were asked whether they had carried a gun while driving in the twelve months prior to the survey and whether they had personally made obscene gestures, cursed or shouted at other drivers, impeded another driver's progress with their vehicle, aggressively "followed another driver too closely," or brandished a gun at another driver. The study found that self-reported hostile behavior while driving was significantly more common among men, young adults, and individuals who carried a firearm in their car. Thus, having a gun in the car was one predictor of aggressive behavior behind the wheel. A subsequent nationwide survey of 2,400 drivers also found that individuals who were in a vehicle with a gun were more likely to display some form of road rage.[53]

There is a view that arming citizens enhances law and order, since the police cannot be present to intervene in all crimes. This view sees armed citizens as a form of auxiliary police force. It is true that police can't be everywhere at the same time; there are about two sworn police officers for every 1,000 residents in the US.[54] However, as we will see in Chapter 5, the training of gun-carrying civilians is nonexistent in many states because about half of the states currently allow people to carry concealed firearms without a permit. In most of the remaining states, the mandated training is considered by experts to be highly inadequate and does not even approach that of sworn officers. It is therefore not surprising that studies find that citizens rarely intervene successfully when violent crimes occur. Victims use guns in fewer than 1 percent of contact crimes.[55] An FBI study of active shooter incidents has found that civilians almost never intervene to thwart the shooter in these cases.[56]

Overall, criminal uses of firearms occur many times more frequently than defensive uses,[57] illustrating that an armed society is a liability rather than a net gain for society. An armed society means that more arguments will escalate to lethal violence. Research shows that arguments and disputes are a major factor in homicides and are even involved in a large number of mass shootings.[58]

More guns are also linked to more fatal shootings of and by the police. One study showed that police officers in high gun ownership states were three times more likely to be killed than officers in low gun ownership states.[59] That study showed that gun ownership seems to be a more powerful factor driving police killings than violent crime rates. Another study found that regions with more gun ownership tended to have both more killings of civilians by police officers as well as more killings of police. The Northeast, the region with the lowest gun ownership levels, had the fewest killings of and by the police, while regions like the South and Southwest, with some of the highest gun ownership levels, ranked high in both police killings and killings of civilians by police.[60] The US also stands alone among advanced nations in the number of civilians killed by the police.[61] For example, the US has *forty times* the German rate of police killings of civilians when population differences are taken into account.[62]

While it is true that there have been many documented killings of unarmed civilians by the police, victims of police shootings often have a gun or an object that looks like a gun in their possession when they are shot, and, in many cases, the subject aimed or discharged a firearm at an officer.[63] While not excusing the large number of police shootings of civilians, the omnipresence of guns in the US leads to an understandable hypervigilance on the part of the police, who are constantly evaluating individuals they stop for a firearm.

Former Seattle police chief Norm Stamper argues that the prevalence of guns in American society contributes to distrust between police departments and the communities they protect. He writes: "Guns make police officers hypervigilant, and a scared cop is a dangerous cop."[64] The widespread availability and carrying of guns in the US creates a climate of fear and distrust since a mistake in underestimating a threat can lead to the death of an officer. A high level of fear and distrust in police-civilian encounters certainly does not promote a polite society.

Myth 6: The Only Consequences of Gun Violence Are Murders

Most debates about the harm produced by gun violence are focused on the physical costs, especially the many tragic deaths arising from gunfire. For example, one question often asked is: Why do we spend so much time discussing mass shootings when these shootings account for just a fraction (about 2 percent) of all gun deaths?

Fact Check: The direct, measurable costs of gun violence in the US are staggering, but there are considerable social, psychological, and economic costs as well.

Physical Harm and Threats to Life

- Firearm deaths in America exceeded 45,000 in 2020,[65] and a total of about 115,000 people are shot each year when fatal and nonfatal injuries are tallied.[66] There have been about 1.5 million gun deaths in the US since 1970, exceeding all deaths from all wars in US history, including the Revolutionary and Civil Wars, the two World Wars, and the wars in Korea, Vietnam, Afghanistan, and Iraq.[67]

- Close to half a million homicides, rapes, assaults, and robberies are committed with guns each year.[68]

- Five million American women have been threatened with a gun by an intimate partner.[69]

Psychological Effects of Gun Violence

Apart from physical costs and threats, survivors of gun attacks often experience intense psychological trauma, as may family members, friends, and colleagues.

The reality of trauma following gun violence is multifaceted. There is the typical emotional trauma following any loss, combined with the impact of the violence that resulted in this loss. Fred Guttenberg, the second author of this book, has often spoken about his daughter Jaime's final seconds and how the sounds of the bullets that took Jaime's life reverberate in his head every second of every day. We wonder, did our loved one die instantly or did they suffer? Did they know what was about to happen or were they spared that anxiety? The emotional aftermath of gun violence often extends far beyond the shooting. Due to the criminal nature of gun violence, a long investigation of facts that causes further trauma to survivors is likely to follow the loss of a loved one in this manner. It is not uncommon for survivors to suffer PTSD as a result. The likelihood of a criminal trial to follow at some point only reinforces that emotional trauma from gun violence is different from other trauma and that its effects are ongoing.

Readers of this book need to look no further than the victim impact statements delivered at the penalty phase for the Parkland shooting trial. For many, as captured by Fred Guttenberg and his wife Jennifer, there is a loss of purpose, as a parent's job is to take care of their children. How do you replace the physical and emotional work that revolves around taking care of your fourteen-year-old child? How do you go forward with the other children in the house who will be forever changed and impacted?

For the very first time, Fred shared the impacts on him and his family, beyond just visiting his daughter at the cemetery. He talked about how the relationship with his son has changed, as anger over what happened is now a part of that relationship. Why anger? That is just one of the many responses to those with survivor's guilt. As the surviving sibling who was also at the school during the shooting, it is normal for him to ask: "Why her and not me? Why did I run to safety and not turn around to do more?"

Says Fred: "It is true that our family, like all families affected by gun violence, is forever changed because of loss. The hopes that we once shared as a family need to be rethought. For me, I won't get to see Jaime graduate high school or college, learn to drive, or have a first boyfriend.

Most importantly, my family won't get to see Jaime get married or become a mother. I will never get to walk my only daughter down the aisle or hold the grandchildren that I will never have."

Jennifer Guttenberg adds:

> It's impossible to describe life without Jaime in the short amount of time that I have been given here, but I will try my best. Every day I live with the fact that Jaime's life was cut too short and was unable to show the world her fullest potential. She missed out on a lifetime of things…high school experiences, dance classes with her friends, high school graduation, moving away to college and college graduation, her first job, getting married, and having kids of her own. The list goes on and on. The pain of this is unbearable. My life feels empty, lonely, and incomplete. There are days that the sadness is so overwhelming, and the crying comes from deep within the gut and causes physical pain. I re-live that day over and over in my mind and can't sleep well. I can't get the thoughts and images of what happened out of my head. My career has suffered, as working with other people's children is now so emotionally taxing. My outlook on life has completely changed in such a negative way. It takes strength just to get through each day. One day at a time we say, even many years later. I lost my daughter, my flesh and blood, the baby that grew inside of me and then, in an instant, she was gone.
>
> I lost my purpose in life that day. My job as a mom to Jaime was taken from me. I went from taking her to dance, going on lunch dates, shopping together, making sure she was fed, healthy, safe, and so much more, to doing nothing. All of our relationships in the house changed that very day, and

we still work hard to repair the damage that this has caused
and to continue moving forward together in a life that is so
drastically different and filled with sadness and trauma.

Bystanders to shootings and mass shootings may also be traumatized as they witness victims bleeding to death and suffering. Following a mass shooting in Killeen, Texas, in 1991, a health team arrived on the scene and interviewed over 130 witnesses and first responders who had not been shot.[70] The team found that nearly a third of those interviewed met the criteria for post-traumatic stress disorder (PTSD) and one in five still struggled with PTSD three years later.

An American Psychological Association survey in 2018 found that mass shootings constituted the greatest source of stress for young people between fifteen and twenty-one years of age.[71] A Morning Consult poll concluded that those born from the mid-1990s on (Gen Z) report that, after the coronavirus pandemic, the issue with the greatest impact on their worldview has been mass shootings, including Sandy Hook, Parkland, and Las Vegas.[72] These events have had a greater impact on them than the terrorist attacks of September 2001 or the Black Lives Matter and "Me Too" movements.

Other Effects of Gun Violence

A Harris poll taken in the summer of 2019 after two high-profile mass shootings in El Paso, Texas, and Dayton, Ohio, found that a third of 2,000 Americans surveyed said their fear was so great that they would avoid going to certain places or events.[73] In turn, such fear has social, psychological, and economic impacts if potential customers and spectators stay home more often due to the possibility of being caught in the middle of a shooting.

Victims of gun violence and their families may incur significant financial losses if they are unable to remain at their jobs, either temporarily or permanently. Physical and psychological therapy may also be required. Financial costs of gun violence to the society or members of the public include medical costs and rehabilitation, criminal justice system costs (police, courts, corrections), and investments in preventing gun violence (alarm systems, private security, weapons purchases, and training).

Sadly, some victims experience life-altering injuries that have a profound impact on their quality of life. For example, when a person is shot and paralyzed in his twenties, his quality of life will be diminished significantly. He may be confined to a wheelchair, suffer pain for the rest of his life, go through countless surgeries, and miss out on the joys of having intimate relationships and having a family. One way of measuring these costs is to examine jury awards for those who have filed lawsuits for damages resulting from gunshot wounds. When all the above financial costs are taken into account, it has been estimated that the annual cost of gun violence in the US is over $280 billion.

Any conversation about gun violence must consider more than the physical toll of shootings. The impact on our lives and communities is far broader than that. Thus, we cannot discuss gun violence and mass shootings with reference to the body count alone. The many ways in which the continuing parade of shootings impacts our society underscores the need for bold action to reduce the number of these tragic events.

Myth 7: Gun Violence Numbers Are Inflated Because They Include Suicides

There are over 40,000 deaths a year (over 100 a day) in the US as a result of gunfire. It is true that over half of these deaths are suicides. It is claimed that gun violence prevention advocates are padding the numbers when they include suicide in the gun violence figures.

Fact Check: First, the World Health Organization considers suicide to be a form of self-directed violence.[74] Second, we do know that many suicides are preventable where lethal means are less accessible. Kay R. Jamison, a psychologist at the Mood Disorders Center of Johns Hopkins University, estimates that just 10–15 percent of suicide cases involve an unwavering determination to die on the part of the victim.[75] For the majority of suicidal people, the risk is transient. Therefore, the presence or absence of highly lethal means of ending one's life, such as firearms, at the time a person is at risk can literally make the difference between life and death.

Therefore, if our focus is on injury prevention, it is entirely legitimate to focus on all preventable gun deaths and injuries, whether these are inflicted on others or oneself or whether the injuries are intentional or unintentional (accidents). Why should we stop at just trying to prevent suffering that results from a crime?

Implicit in the argument made by those opposed to counting suicides is the moralistic argument that someone who attempts suicide should not be our concern and somehow deserves their fate. We share the public health community's view that helping those on the precipice of taking their own lives is something positive that strengthens the ties that bind us. This is especially the case when reducing access to lethal methods can make a difference in many cases, as individuals attempting suicide often do not repeat their attempts.

Furthermore, even if we set suicide aside, the US stands alone among high-income countries with a gun homicide rate that is twenty-five times that of the aggregate rate of other high-income countries.[76]

Myth 8: Guns Make Women Safer

There is a belief that a gun will protect women from men who may prey on them. Guns are viewed by some as a great equalizer, as they are said to compensate for the smaller physical stature of women.

Fact Check: When we examine violence against women, it quickly becomes apparent that most violence against women is committed in private by male partners rather than in public spaces by strangers. Over nine in ten of women who are murdered are killed by men they know, and the majority of those men are intimate partners. Guns are the weapon used in more than half of all killings of women. Given that much violence against women is committed by intimate partners, guns kept by women in the home may be used against them. Here is some evidence showing that guns are more likely to be a threat than a source of protection for women:

- One study shows that women living with a gun in the home are three times more likely to be murdered than are women with no guns in the home.[77]

- A study of California adults (mostly women) who began living with handgun owners between 2004 and 2016 found that cohabitants of these owners were seven times as likely to be fatally shot by a spouse or intimate partner as those living with non-handgun owners.[78]

- A homicide is eight times more likely to occur when an abuser has access to a firearm.[79]

- While close to 800 American women are murdered each year by men with guns, just a dozen or so women use a gun to commit a justifiable homicide against a man.[80]

- One study found that women in states with higher gun ownership rates were several times more likely to be murdered by a gun than women in states with lower gun ownership rates.[81]

- Women who are murdered are more rather than less likely to have purchased a handgun in the three-year period prior to their deaths, illustrating that the guns purchased were more likely to harm than protect them.[82]

- Many women report that guns have been used by abusers to threaten and intimidate them. The trauma experienced by women who have been abused is more severe when gun-related threats have been part of the abuse.[83]

- Author Evan DeFilippis writes: "…[N]ot a single study to date has shown that the risk of any crime, including burglary, robbery, home invasion, or spousal abuse against a female, is decreased through gun ownership." DeFilippis adds:

Christy Salters Martin is a professional boxer and the owner of a concealed carry permit. But when she attempted to leave her husband, she was shot with her own gun. Today, she cautions other women against making the same mistake.

*Just putting a weapon in the woman's hand is not going to
reduce the number of fatalities or gunshot victims that we
have. Too many times, their male counterpart or spouse will
be able to overpower them and take that gun away.*[84]

Despite aggressive efforts on the part of the gun industry to market guns
to women, the vast majority of women are not interested in owning and
carrying guns; even though there has been a surge in gun ownership
in America during the pandemic, just one in five women are gun
owners.[85] In general, women do not want guns and female teachers are
overwhelmingly opposed to gun possession by school staff.

Myth 9: Arming Teachers Will Make Schools Safer

Following the slaughter of students and school staff at both Sandy Hook
Elementary School in Newtown, Connecticut, and Marjory Stoneman
Douglas High School in Parkland, Florida, there were calls by the NRA to
arm teachers. Wayne LaPierre's oft-repeated slogan, "The only thing that
stops a bad guy with a gun is a good guy with a gun," was first said by him
after the Newtown shooting. The NRA went on to use the Newtown mass
shooting to push for additional gun sales, and they have been successful.
After the Parkland mass shooting, Florida passed a law allowing school
districts to train and arm school staff.

Fact Check: The recitation of LaPierre's slogan in the aftermath of these
slaughters of our young is in our view cynical, offensive, and unsupported
by empirical evidence. It is also as illogical to suggest that increasing the
volume of guns will reduce gun violence as it is to make opioids more
accessible as a way of addressing the opioid crisis. The proposed solution
of arming teachers is highly cynical as this measure is presented as the
last line of defense keeping schools from descending into complete chaos.

While schools have their challenges and have seen more violence during the pandemic, there is hardly an epidemic of active shooter incidents in schools that would justify such a draconian response. The FBI has found forty-four active shooter incidents in twenty years in Pre-K-12 schools or an average of two such incidents a year in the more than 130,000 public and private schools in the US.[86] We are very far from descending into chaos in the schools.

The absurdity of arming teachers as the principal means of combatting school shootings should be evident following the horrific massacre of twenty-one schoolchildren and staff (with seventeen more injured) at Robb Elementary School in Uvalde, Texas, on May 24, 2022.[87] Officers from six law enforcement agencies responded, and many wore bulletproof vests, carried shields, and were armed with assault-style weapons. The shooter also wore body armor and possessed an AR-15 style rifle. Video footage showed that the shooter repelled a number of officers by firing several rounds in the hallway and then proceeded to murder the children in a classroom while the officers remained in the corridor for seventy-seven minutes. The failure of armed security to engage a shooter also was seen in the 2018 high school mass shooting in Parkland, Florida. It is difficult to envision schoolteachers with handguns thwarting a determined shooter with body armor, an assault-style rifle, and hundreds of rounds of ammunition.

Arming teachers or school staff also completely fails to address the reasons why so many young men in America, relative to other countries, appear ready to murder as many of their peers as possible, nor does this proposal address the accessibility of weapons that enable these massacres. Arming teachers does nothing to stop those who intend violence from planning an attack, acquiring weapons and ammunition, and carrying out a mass shooting event. In the case of Parkland, had the on-campus armed law enforcement officer taken action and done something, perhaps he could have reduced the carnage, but he would not have been able to stop it. Perhaps Jaime Guttenberg, who was killed on the third floor, the second to last or thirty-third person to be shot, could have been saved. But how many would still have been killed or wounded? While we will never know, our second author Fred Guttenberg has seen the photos and videos of the shooting in progress; he has seen the chaos they captured. If panicked and armed teachers had been shooting into the running crowds of students trying to get to safety, more people might in fact have ended up being shot.

Students in large numbers walk from school campuses to waiting cars and buses every day. Jaime's brother walked out to the car every day with his sister. What if the determined shooter had been waiting outside the campus? Such a situation may have produced even more casualties, and armed teachers would have been of little use in stopping that.

Surveys show that neither teachers nor the public like the idea.[88] Like their college and university counterparts, most educators are not interested in doubling as security guards, and students would feel less safe with schools awash in guns. Teachers worry about undermining their special role as educators and mentors, which consists of a different skill set from that of security staff. School teachers are usually women,[89] and women tend to have low gun ownership levels. Schools would likely lose valuable talent. Even if just some teachers were armed, incentives would likely be required to recruit and retain teachers with weapons training, creating a preference for those prepared to undergo the necessary training over talent in the classroom. In addition, at a time when teachers are often compelled to buy school supplies for their students from their own funds,[90] scarce educational resources will be diverted from the classroom to firearms training.

The cost of training teachers and/or other school staff willing to serve as armed marshals would be prohibitive, and ongoing training and recertification would require time out of class, with additional associated costs. After Kansas gave school districts the prerogative of arming teachers, the state's largest insurer of schools refused to cover schools with armed instructors, deeming the situation unduly risky.[91]

In general, experts note that even in states where a permit is required to carry a gun, the training required to obtain a permit is woefully inadequate. Rigorous training ought to include instruction in the law pertaining to the use of force, gun safety and handling, judgment (when to shoot and not to shoot), awareness of the possibility of friendly fire incidents, and marksmanship under stress. Even trained police officers miss their targets about 80 percent of the time in combat situations. Deployment of a gun in a crowded school being attacked by a shooter requires exceptional skill, judgment, and composure.

While there are far too many school shootings in the US relative to other countries, it is generally only in relation to active shooter incidents—a shooting in progress—that armed school staff could theoretically intervene. There is no opportunity to intercede where a student draws a gun and fires during a spontaneous dispute. As indicated above, there is an average of approximately two active shooter incidents per year in 130,000 US schools. Thus, one in every 65,000 schools experiences such an event each year.

Do these rare but tragic events justify the arming of teachers or other staff? Just as in the case of firearms kept in the home, arming teachers in every school may well result in many more unforeseen misuses of firearms rather than uses in which lives are saved. Downsides of such a policy include unauthorized uses of force, accidental shootings and discharges, and thefts of guns. Teachers may over-react in dealing with unruly students and use deadly force to control them, a departure from the intent of arming them. Issues relating to the disproportionate use of firearms against minority students may arise, as this is already an issue with full-time, professionally trained law enforcement officers.[92]

To illustrate what could go wrong if teachers around the country were armed, consider a forty-eight-hour period in March, 2018, during which three mishaps with guns occurred.[93] A Virginia school police officer accidentally fired his gun in his office, sending a bullet through a wall into a middle school classroom. A teacher demonstrating firearms safety in California mistakenly put a round into the ceiling, injuring three students who were hit by falling debris. And a veteran sheriff left a loaded service weapon in a locker room at a Michigan middle school, where a sixth grader found it. Two of these cases involved law enforcement officers; therefore, what would happen if more teachers were armed? Also, one suspects that many such cases are never reported or documented. Many school employees say they would feel less safe if more of their colleagues were carrying weapons.[94]

Experience with active shooter situations indicates that many could not be stopped by armed school personnel. Even if they could, the number of accidents and inappropriate uses of firearms by school personnel would exceed by a wide margin the lives saved and injuries prevented by armed school personnel. There are far more constructive (and less dangerous) ways of preventing shootings in the school than responding to incidents in progress with inadequately trained school personnel.

Myth 10: Gun Violence Is Just a Problem in the Inner Cities

This view suggests that we need not worry about gun violence and mass shootings if we live in the suburbs, small towns, or rural areas. The statement may also be interpreted as coded language suggesting that gun violence is limited to communities of color in urban areas and therefore does not merit our attention.

Fact Check: According to a survey conducted in 2018, 58 percent of American adults report that they or someone they care for have experienced gun violence at some point in their life.[95] The same survey found that one in four American adults have personally been threatened or intimidated with a gun. Such findings contradict the notion that gun violence is quite rare and affects just a small segment of the population, mostly those living in disadvantaged urban areas. The view that most gun violence occurs in urban areas can give people outside those areas a false sense of security and keep us from addressing the full scope of the problem. And, obviously, we should reject any implication that some citizens are somehow more worthy of attention than others.

While homicide rates are higher in large cities than small towns,[96] the notion that gun violence is just a problem in large cities is incorrect. For example, recent experience with mass shootings shows that no venue is immune from gun violence. Over the last few years, we have seen shootings at concerts, in places of worship, in schools and on college campuses, as well as in nightclubs, movie theaters, airports, malls, and every other type of venue. Many of America's most horrific mass shootings have occurred in small towns or suburbs rather than inner cities. These include the school shootings at Columbine High School, Sandy Hook Elementary School, and Marjory Stonemen Douglas High School, the shootings on the campus of Virginia Tech, the church shooting in Sutherland Springs, Texas, and the movie theater shooting in Aurora, Colorado. The shooters in many of America's deadliest mass shootings have been young white men rather than persons of color.

In the US as a whole, over 80 percent of the population lives in an urban area.[97] The ten states with the highest firearms death rates in 2019 all have a level of urbanization that is lower than the national average (i.e., less than 80 percent of their populations live in an urban area). In fact, in three of the states with the highest gun death rates—Alabama, Arkansas, and Mississippi—less than 60 percent of the population lives in an urban area.[98] Thus, rural areas too can have high rates of gun death. In fact, a study covering 2016–2020 found that thirteen of the twenty US counties with the most gun homicides per capita were rural and that, in 2020, the total gun death rate per 100,000 people was 40 percent higher in rural communities than it was in large metropolitan areas.[99]

However, state gun death rates increase with gun ownership levels. Nine of the ten states with the highest gun mortality rates have about a 20 percent higher household gun ownership rate than the ownership rate for the country as a whole.[100] An analysis conducted by the first author in his book *Confronting Gun Violence in America* found that the ten states with the weakest gun laws had over twice the gun death rate as the ten states with the strongest gun laws.[101] Thus, gun deaths are linked more closely to gun ownership and weak gun laws than they are to urban living.

Guns and Public Safety: The Bottom Line

- The scientific evidence shows that an armed society is a more dangerous society and not a more polite one. The US stands out among high-income countries both in its high levels of gun ownership and gun-related mortality. A high percentage of Americans have been touched by violence, either directly or indirectly. The high volume of firearms among civilians in America creates a number of side effects, including the undermining of law and order. Research shows that as gun ownership levels rise, so do fatal shootings of police officers by civilians and of civilians by the police. More shootings of police lead to even more suspicion and hypervigilance on the part of the police, which can lead to more human rights abuses and fatal shootings by nervous police officers. More shootings of civilians can result in social unrest, especially when these shootings occur disproportionately against identifiable groups. Therefore, arming more civilians not only makes for a more dangerous society, but a less stable and cohesive one as well.

• Some measure the impact of gun violence solely by its physical costs. However, gun violence represents more than a threat to life and limb. Those experiencing violence and surviving it, those witnessing it, and those who have lost a loved one may experience lifelong psychological effects. Polls also show that many Americans are limiting some of their social activities due to the fear of gun violence and mass shootings. In addition, the economic costs of gun violence are enormous, including direct medical costs, rehabilitation, lost income, criminal justice system costs, the costs of crime prevention, and quality of life costs.

• Counting suicides as part of the toll of gun violence is not inflating the numbers. Suicide, which is considered a form of self-directed violence by the global health community, is a legitimate focus of strategies designed to prevent gun-related injuries. Many fatalities and severe injuries could be prevented by reducing the access of teenagers and at-risk adults to firearms. Many of those who attempt suicide and survive will not repeat the attempt, hence, reducing access to more lethal methods such as firearms will save lives.

• Guns are far more likely to be used against women, especially by an abuser or former partner, than to be used by women in self-defense. Women have far more to fear from intimate partners than from strangers. Intimate partners who have access to guns pose far more of a threat to women than those without such access because guns are more likely to escalate abuse to a homicide. When guns are used by abusers to threaten women, the trauma developed in reaction to the abuse is intensified.

- Arming teachers would have few upsides and many downsides. Most acts of violence in schools are not of the active shooter type and are over in a matter of a few seconds. Armed school staff would have little opportunity to intervene in time. On the downside, placing guns in the hands of civilians in schools will produce more gun misuses that will far outnumber any benefit, including inappropriate uses of force, suicides, accidental discharges, and gun thefts. Teachers overwhelmingly oppose the idea of being armed, and resources would be wasted on firearms training rather than investing them in teaching and school supplies. The extensive training required to prepare armed teachers to confront a shooter with students around would not only be very costly but would likely be inadequate. Intervening in an active shooter situation is the work of SWAT teams rather than teachers. Any possible benefit would be outweighed by the change in the teacher's role from one of educator to that of security provider in a militarized zone.

- The belief that gun violence is largely confined to disadvantaged areas in major cities is incorrect. The large number of Americans touched by gun violence attests to the fact that it is an issue throughout the country, including in rural areas. States with high rural versus urban populations often have higher gun mortality rates than more urbanized states, and many of the country's worst mass shootings have occurred in small towns and suburbs rather than urban centers. In part, this can be explained by higher levels of gun ownership in more rural states. Gun violence is an American problem, not merely an urban one.

Chapter 4

THE TRUTH ABOUT GUNS AND ASSAULT WEAPONS

Myth 11: Guns Don't Kill People, People Kill People

One of the best-known slogans coming from gun rights advocates conveys the superficial truth that it is people, not the weapon, who kill. Following a string of high casualty mass shootings in the spring and summer of 2022 involving AR-15 style firearms, executives from two gun manufacturers stated at a Congressional committee hearing that firearms were "inanimate objects" and that these horrors were rooted in local problems and had nothing to do with the weapon used.[102] Those who hold this belief assume that the weapon is easily replaced by some other tool to achieve the aims of the assailant. Perpetrators are viewed as "bad" actors who plan their attacks and have an unwavering determination to kill. Those holding this view believe that any restrictions on guns are futile as another means will be found to kill if guns are not available.

Fact Check: Those opposing restrictions on guns subscribe to a simplistic, single-dimensional view of gun violence. If all acts of violence involved an unwavering desire to kill, then we might agree that the weapon used, whether a gun, knife, or blunt instrument, might be less critical since the person would continue to try to kill their target(s) until they succeeded. The truth is, however, that the overwhelming majority of acts of violence are not intended to kill but may result in death due to the use of lethal weapons.

In addition, this narrow view of violence ignores the many acts of violence that arise spontaneously. Often, individuals display issues with managing their anger and react impulsively to perceived slights or provocations. Where violence erupts suddenly, anger may also dissipate quickly. In these cases, the absence of a gun may prevent a killing as the attacker was not contemplating killing in advance.

To many of those advocating the ownership of guns for self-defense, the world is black and white and we are all either "good guys" or "bad guys." In such dualistic framing, it is either the person or the gun that is dangerous. Here's a posting by a reader in response to a gun violence blogger: "Maybe if the idiots spouting gun control would put criminals in jail for the shootings…that would make a difference. I have yet to see a firearm jump up on its own and pull the trigger by itself without a human being pulling the trigger!"[103]

People like the author of this quote don't consider the fact that both the inclinations of the person and the availability of the weapon are influential in the outcome of a violent attack. They don't entertain the idea that the world is more complex and that people with guns may be more dangerous than the same people without guns or that a "good guy" today with no criminal record may be a mass shooter tomorrow.

It is also a contradiction that armed self-defense advocates view a gun as irrelevant and easily replaceable when it is in the hands of an aggressor but sacred and effective when it comes to self-defense. You can't have it both ways. If guns are more lethal than other tools when they are in the hands of those defending themselves, they will also be more lethal than other instruments when used by an aggressor.

If the tool is irrelevant, we can save billions of dollars a year by equipping the military and law enforcement with hammers rather than guns. Musician Ozzy Osbourne grasped the absurdity of the argument that the weapon doesn't matter when he said: "I keep hearing this [expletive] thing that guns don't kill people, but people kill people. If that's the case, why do we give people guns when they go to war? Why not just send the people?"[104]

To illustrate that guns influence the seriousness of injuries independent of the intent of an aggressor or suicidal individual, consider the laws of physics and how they apply to the danger posed by any weapon, be it a gun or a fist. Dr. Arthur Kellermann, formerly an emergency room physician and the founding chairman of Emory University's Department of Emergency Medicine, has been one of the most influential researchers on the risks posed by guns. Kellermann and his colleagues made the following observations on the factors that make guns and ammunition more or less lethal:

> The specific capacity of a firearm to cause injury depends on its accuracy, the rate of fire, muzzle velocity, and specific characteristics of the projectile [bullet]...Weapons with high muzzle velocities, e.g., hunting rifles, generally cause greater tissue damage than weapons with lower muzzle velocities, e.g., handguns. However, the size, shape, and nature of the projectile also play a powerful role in determining the severity of the resultant injury. ...A slower bullet, designed to mushroom or fragment on impact, may damage a much larger amount of tissue through direct trauma, cavitation, and shock wave effects. ...Damage also increases in direct

proportion to the mass of the projectile. The number of
projectiles striking the body also influences the expected
severity of injury.[105]

Kellermann and his colleagues added that some gunshot wounds are so extensive that survival is unlikely. Thus, emergency room doctors who routinely deal with gunshot wounds confirm the commonsense notion that firearms vary greatly in their lethality, independent of the intent of the shooter. The same laws of physics indicate that the danger posed by guns will differ from the hazards associated with other categories of weapons, such as knives, sticks, or fists.

There is considerable evidence that weapons do matter in the case of homicide. Guns facilitate homicide in a number of ways:

Gun Attacks Are More Lethal Than Attacks with Other Weapons

The most obvious way guns can facilitate killing is that they are more lethal than other weapons. The presence of firearms may make disputes, assaults, or robberies more deadly. Whether the offense is committed by a calculating, cold-blooded killer or by an individual exhibiting rage, there is strong evidence showing that firearms are more lethal than other weapons. Professionals in the medical field have noted the damage to humans produced by high-velocity weapons that fire larger bullets designed to cause severe injuries. Back in the 1960s, surgeons Robert Richter and Mahfouz Zaki of Brooklyn, New York, compared the damage inflicted by guns as opposed to knives:

If the velocity of a knife at the moment of stabbing is
estimated at 30 miles per hour (the actual figure may
be lower), that value is 18 times smaller than the muzzle
velocity of a 25-caliber pistol bullet used in commercially

available guns. … One must simply expect that a far greater
proportion of bullet wounds inflict serious damage than do
stab wounds.[106]

Firearms available widely today are far more lethal than they were when the above passage was written. Bullets from an AR-15 travel at about 3,000 feet per second when they exit the rifle, which is many times faster than the rate of bullets from the pistol described above. If guns and ammunition vary in their lethality, it is hardly credible to argue that entirely different categories of weapons (guns vs. knives or clubs) will cause the same damage.

Consider an influential study of robberies (including holdups and muggings) in forty-three US cities by Philip Cook of Duke University.[107] His study found a strong link between the weapon used and the likelihood of a fatal outcome. In gun robberies, there was a fatality in one in every 250 incidents. This was three times greater than the likelihood of death in a knife robbery and nine times greater than the likelihood of death where other weapons were used. The lowest death rates were found in unarmed robberies (one in every 5,000 incidents). Robberies involving firearms were twenty times more likely to result in a death than were unarmed robberies.

Are these significant differences in lethality due to the more lethal intent of gun robbers or due to the differential dangerousness of the weapons used—the *instrumentality* effect? The crime of robbery provides an excellent opportunity to examine this question because robbers almost never set out to kill their victims. Deaths in robberies, even gun robberies, are rare. Rather than using guns to kill their victims, robbers tend to choose guns in order to gain the quick compliance of their victims and to *avoid* violence. Their aim is to obtain cash and exit the crime scene as quickly as possible, since delay is likely to lead to their arrest and a possible confrontation with police or witnesses. As most robberies involve minimal planning, the choice of a weapon has less to do with personality or intent and more to do with the availability of guns when the decision is made to commit a robbery.

Violence is actually more likely to occur when robbers are unarmed as the victim is more likely to resist the robber.[108] Even so, fatalities are far more likely to occur when guns are used, since the slightest hesitation on the part of a victim, or even the intervention of a bystander, may lead a nervous robber to take the irrevocable decision to discharge his weapon.

In a classic study conducted in the late 1960s, Franklin Zimring, then a University of Chicago law professor, used an innovative methodology to isolate the impact of the weapon on the outcome of assaults. Reviewing Chicago Police data for 1967, he found that assaults with firearms were five times as likely to result in the victim's death as knife attacks.[109] He anticipated that critics would attribute this finding to a greater intent to kill on the part of those attacking with guns, rather than the greater lethality of guns versus knives. However, Zimring showed that the type of people involved in the attacks, as well as their motives and circumstances of the assaults, were very similar in gun and knife attacks. To further dispel the idea that knife assailants are less determined to kill, he examined the location of all the knife and gun wounds and found that, in fact, a higher percentage of knife as opposed to gunshot wounds were in vital regions of the body (head, chest, abdomen, back, and neck). When he compared gun attacks with only the most serious knife attacks (those directed to the victim's vital regions), he found that gun attacks were still two and a half times more likely to kill than knife attacks. Therefore, the study strongly pointed to the conclusion that the difference in lethality between gun and knife attacks was due to the greater dangerousness of guns rather than to the more lethal intent of those using guns.

Guns Enable Mass Casualty Incidents

It is hard to envision the murder of large numbers of people with knives, clubs, fists, and other instruments that are not firearms. While such events have been known to occur, the vast majority of mass killings, high-profile school killings, and workplace killings in the US are committed with firearms, and nearly all are committed by one person.[110] The lack of accomplices in many incidents, the speedy response by law enforcement agencies, and the possible intervention of bystanders make it almost imperative for a perpetrator bent on inflicting mass casualties to use firearms capable of discharging a large number of rounds of ammunition in a short period of time.

Self-loading firearms in particular, whether automatic or semiautomatic, allow just one individual to kill and seriously injure dozens of people even where the police respond within minutes. For example, on July 20, 2012, one shooter using as one of his weapons an AR-15 magazine-fed, semiautomatic rifle, shot seventy-one people in less than five minutes in a Colorado movie theater. On August 4, 2019, thirty-five people were shot in under thirty seconds in Dayton, Ohio's Oregon entertainment district. The shooter used an AR-15 style rifle equipped with a drum magazine holding 100 rounds of ammunition. Police officers patrolling the district responded within minutes.

Dayton's police chief, Richard Biehl, had the following to say about the futility of the rapid response by his officers to the 2019 shooting in the city's Oregon District:

> *Despite their best efforts, their heroic efforts, their*
> *extraordinarily rapid response to this horrific threat doing*
> *what has really rarely been done anywhere in the country*
> *to stop a threat that soon, and still nine dead and 20*
> *others injured...It's amazing the harm a person can cause*

in such an extraordinarily short period of time when they
have a high-velocity weapon with an enormous amount
of ammunition...There's a balance between protecting
oneself and providing weapons and equipment that allows
mass shootings to occur and for victims to be injured or
killed at a rate of more than 1 per second, which happened
in the Oregon district...That's unconscionable and that's
something that can't be deemed reasonable.[111]

Firearms Are Needed to Kill or Rob Armed or Protected Targets

Attacks on political figures or police officers without firearms will likely leave the assailant outgunned. Similarly, robberies targeting well-guarded facilities and transports such as armored trucks are not likely to be successful without firearms or replica firearms. Most political assassinations and all American presidential assassinations (Lincoln, Garfield, McKinley, and Kennedy) have involved firearms. Police officers are almost always killed with a gun when they are the targets of homicide. In 2021, of law enforcement officers killed on duty, sixty-one were shot, whereas four were beaten and three were stabbed to death.[112] The lesson learned here is that guns are difficult to replace in the commission of certain crimes.

Guns Allow Killing by the Physically Vulnerable or the Squeamish

Guns may facilitate killing by minors, the disabled, or others who would otherwise be incapable of inflicting serious damage upon others. In this way, they can be viewed as an equalizer.[113] Guns can also provide an impersonal means of killing for those who are too squeamish to sever another's arteries with a sharp instrument or fracture someone's skull with a heavy, blunt instrument.[114]

Guns Facilitate Killing from a Distance

Guns allow killing and wounding from a distance, such as drive-by killings and sniper murders. Drive-by stabbings are hard to envision. In 2002, Beltway snipers John Allen Muhammad and Lee Boyd Malvo killed ten people and terrorized residents of Washington, DC, Maryland, and Virginia with an armed crime spree.[115] They equipped their Chevrolet Caprice with a firing port through which they could shoot people at random without being detected. Their crimes could not have been committed without a firearm. Both Bushmaster, the manufacturer of the weapon used, and the gun store that sold it without maintaining records were sued by some of the victims' families and eventually paid out a sum of money to settle the case out of court.

There have also been a number of cases in which individuals have been shot randomly on freeways or have been shot in road rage incidents. In August and September 2015, ten shootings occurred on the I-10 highway and one on the I-17 highway in Phoenix, Arizona. Eight of the vehicles were struck by bullets and three by unspecified projectiles.[116] While other objects can be hurled at vehicles, none have the range and lethality of projectiles from firearms.

Guns Can Endanger Innocent Bystanders

Innocent bystanders are far more likely to be hurt or killed in a gun attack than an attack involving other types of weapons. In a 2015 road rage incident in Albuquerque, New Mexico, two vehicles cut each other off on the I-40 highway. One driver then pulled alongside the other and opened fire; the second driver's four-year-old daughter was killed.[117] In another example, a man driving in Orlando, Florida, was caught in the crossfire as some sort of shooting was taking place in that neighborhood.[118]

Guns Facilitate Impulsive Killings

Where attacks have been carefully planned, the perpetrator may well proceed, regardless of whether a specific type of weapon is available. Where an attack is more impulsive, the presence or absence of lethal weapons is all-important. Guns are unique in that, once the trigger is pulled, harm will occur if the target is hit. With knives, blunt instruments, or fists, the user may reconsider and pull back from the brink by aborting an attack or softening a punch, blow, or stabbing movement. Some researchers have noted that the outcome of domestic violence is especially influenced by the availability of lethal weapons. While spousal abuse is often repetitive, abusers tend to be impulsive and volatile. The presence of a firearm during violent episodes has been found to increase the chances that an assault against a partner will result in a fatality.[119] Youth homicide, too, is strongly influenced by the presence of guns since much youth violence is impulsive in nature.

Guns May Precipitate Aggression: The Weapons Effect

An interesting line of inquiry suggests that guns by their mere presence may "trigger" aggressive actions when people are mildly angered. In pioneering work in the 1960s, social psychologist Leonard Berkowitz tested the question of whether "the trigger pulls the finger" in addition to the reverse. Berkowitz and his colleague conducted an experiment in which men were provoked to anger and given an opportunity to administer mild shocks to an accomplice of the researcher. The study found that the men who were provoked to anger and then saw firearms on a nearby table struck back harder at the accomplice than did the men who got angry and saw neutral objects or no objects at all on the table next to the shock apparatus.[120] Berkowitz believed that the mere sight of the guns stimulated the angered men to give their antagonists more shocks. In his view, visual cues such as firearms can evoke a conditioned aggressive response because they have been previously associated with aggression.

Recent work by Jennifer Klinesmith and her colleagues at Knox College in Illinois found another explanation for such an effect.[121] Male students had their testosterone levels measured prior to the experiment. Students in one group were then encouraged to handle a gun, while the other group played a game. Subsequent measurement of their testosterone levels found that those handling the gun had a greater increase in their testosterone levels. Each group was then given an opportunity to engage in aggressive behavior, and those who had handled the gun displayed more aggression. Furthermore, those showing greater increases in testosterone level showed more aggressive behavior than others. The study suggests that the presence of guns may produce hormonal changes in males that then elicit aggressive behavior.

The fact that weapons matter is illustrated by the finding that mass shootings involving assault-style rifles equipped with high-capacity magazines usually produce far more casualties (including both deaths and nonfatal injuries) than when other firearms are used.[122] In addition, studies are finding that semiautomatic handguns with magazines with capacities of ten rounds or higher tend to produce more bullet holes in victims and hence are more lethal. The average person killed by a firearm in Chicago in 2016 was struck by twice as many bullets as one killed in 1992—about four rounds on average as opposed to two. This has been attributed to the increasing ubiquity of semiautomatic pistols with magazines holding ten or more rounds of ammunition.[123]

As seen in Chapter 3, places with more guns tend to have more gun deaths, indicating some form of connection between guns and death. If weapons had no impact on public safety, places with more guns should have no more deaths than places with fewer guns. After all, according to that logic, the number of guns in circulation is irrelevant; it is only people and their motives that count. Countries and states with more guns do however tend to have more gun deaths, indicating that these instruments, independent of other factors, do have an adverse impact on the public's well-being.

Myth 12: An AR-15-Style Rifle Is a Sporting Gun

Fact Check: Faced with the recurring threat of another federal assault weapons ban, the gun lobby and industry began to refer to guns like the AR-15 as a "sporting gun." ArmaLite, Inc. first developed the AR-15 in the 1950s as a military rifle but sold the design to Colt after they had little success selling it.[124] In the 1960s, the US military selected Colt to manufacture the automatic rifle (machine gun) used by US troops in Vietnam. This rifle, based on the design for the AR-15, was known as the M-16. Following that success, Colt ramped up production of a semiautomatic version of the M-16 for law enforcement and the public, marketing it as the AR-15. When Colt's patents for the AR-15 expired in the 1970s, other gunmakers created similar models. AR-15 is now the generic term for these firearms. Jim Sullivan helped design the AR-15. Responding to questions about the role of these firearms in a civilian context, he stated: "Of course, everybody gets concerned when there's one of these school issues where children are killed by an AR-15. I mean, that's sickening. But that was never the intended purpose. Civilian sales were never the intended purpose."[125]

Mike Weisser, a nationally recognized gun expert and trainer, points out that some of the most popular handguns sold in the US have been produced for the military, not for sport, by manufacturers like Glock, SigArms, and Beretta.[126] Weisser states that the US is the only advanced country that fails to restrict weapons of war like the AR-15 style rifles. He says that the only difference between these rifles and the M-16 used by the military is that the civilian version is modified to fire in semiautomatic mode only.[127] That is, the trigger must be pulled to fire each round, whereas fully automatic firearms will fire until the shooter releases the trigger or until all rounds are exhausted. Other than the mode of fire (automatic versus semiautomatic), the civilian version is just as lethal.

The gun industry used the differences in firing modes to claim that the civilian version is a "sporting gun" because it fires in semiautomatic mode only. However, the military now believes that a semiautomatic rifle is more appropriate in certain tactical situations. In addition, Weisser says the following about the similarity in lethality of the civilian and military versions of these rifles:

> And if anyone believes that an AR-15 in semi-auto mode isn't almost as lethal as a rifle that delivers firepower in full-auto mode, then such a belief simply reflects how such individuals misunderstand how the AR-15 is designed and used. To begin with, both the military and civilian versions of the assault gun have a radically different internal design which creates a much quicker movement of the bolt and therefore means that the semi-auto delivery of each round is much faster than what occurs in the semi-auto bolt action in most other semi-auto guns...The kid who murdered 26 adults and children at the Sandy Hook Elementary School using an AR-15 needed less than three minutes of firing time to blast out more than 90 rounds. Additionally, not only does the gun load from the bottom of the frame, which allows the shooter to use a magazine of almost unlimited size and capacity, but the mechanism which releases an empty magazine and locks in a loaded magazine also operates much more quickly than other bottom-loading guns. Taken together, these design features, as well as the light weight of the gun which makes it more maneuverable

in small spaces like a small room or hallway, makes the so-called "modern sporting gun" as lethal as any gun could be, regardless of firing mode.[128]

The Role of Firearms and Assault Weapons in Catalyzing Violence: The Bottom Line

The slogan, "Guns don't kill people, people kill people," creates a false choice: Either it is the person and his malign motives or the presence of guns that is responsible for killing. Why can't it be some combination of the two? While it is people who pull the trigger, guns are a more lethal tool than knives, clubs, and other weapons normally available to people.

Emergency room physicians observe firsthand the damage different guns produce and point out that the laws of physics apply to the harm inflicted by guns versus other weapons. For example, bullets hit their targets at far higher velocities than knives or blunt instruments, and certain firearms, such as the AR-15, have muzzle velocities of about 3,000 feet per second. The damage inflicted by projectiles traveling at such velocities is well beyond the damage produced by an individual wielding a knife or blunt instrument though other considerations, such as the mass of a bullet, are also important.

Guns enable homicide in the following ways:

- Gun attacks are more lethal than attacks with other weapons

- Guns enable mass casualty incidents

- Firearms are needed to rob or kill armed or protected targets

- Guns allow killing by the physically vulnerable

- Guns allow killing at a distance

- Guns can endanger innocent bystanders

- Guns enable impulsive killings committed in a fit of rage where the shooter had no intention to kill the victim

- Guns may even precipitate aggression through the "weapons effect"

There are about 20 million AR-15-style rifles in civilian hands in the US.[129] These weapons are especially lethal and were designed for military uses. They are not sporting guns. The US is the only advanced country that fails to restrict such weapons. They are suited for mass casualty slayings because such weapons are designed to fire more rapidly than other firearms available to civilians. They can also be fed by high-capacity magazines, limiting the number of times a shooter must reload, though these weapons are also designed for rapid reloading.

Chapter 5

THE TRUTH ABOUT GUNS AND SELF-DEFENSE

Myth 13: Guns Provide a Net Benefit to Society in That They Are More Likely to Be Used for Protection Than to Commit Crimes

Fact Check: If guns truly provided a net benefit to society, countries and regions with more guns and weaker gun laws would be safer than places with fewer guns and more restrictions on firearms. The gun lobby and a small group of researchers have promoted the notion of an armed citizenry. Recall that after the Sandy Hook Elementary School mass shooting in Connecticut, Wayne LaPierre of the NRA stated: "The only thing that stops a bad guy with a gun is a good guy with a gun." The studies that have claimed that the beneficial or defensive uses of firearms outnumber harmful uses have been profoundly discredited (see examination of Kleck's research below).

First, consider the logic (or lack thereof) of claiming that defensive gun uses outnumber criminal or aggressive uses. Suppose a researcher conducted a survey asking people about the number of times (if any) over the previous year when they had been threatened or attacked with a gun and the number of times (if any) when they used a gun in self-defense. Based on this survey, the researcher claims that there were a million cases in which guns were used in self-defense and half a million cases in which they were used in a criminal or aggressive fashion. But how can this be possible? He would be saying that there had been a half million more cases of defensive than criminal uses, and therefore a half million cases in which people said they used a gun in self-defense against someone not armed with a gun!

Is it really a legitimate act of self-defense when a person uses a gun to fend off an unarmed individual? According to the English legal tradition which forms the basis for American law, acts of self-defense are only deemed to be lawful if they were proportional to the threat. Armed self-defense against an unarmed aggressor has generally been considered to be an excessive response. While it can be argued that a person using a firearm against a much larger adversary is acting in self-defense, there are many acts of aggression with a gun that are never reported to a survey, so these are seriously undercounted. Victims of domestic violence may face numerous threats of gun violence at the hands of an abuser and may fail to report these due to fear of reprisal, a sense of shame, or their minimization of these actions.

Studies have shown that people involved in disputes often claim they were acting in self-defense when they were full participants in a dispute. Five criminal court judges evaluated thirty-five different descriptions of reported self-defense uses of guns by participants in two Harvard University surveys. In over half the cases, the majority of judges rated the purported self-defense actions as "probably illegal."[130]

If guns provided a net benefit to society, the US, which has the largest armed civilian population in the world (120 guns for every 100 people), ought to be among the safest societies on the planet. Instead, this country has twenty-five times the gun homicide rate as all the other high-income countries considered together. And women and children are far more likely to be killed with guns in the US when compared with other high-income countries.[131]

Tom Gabor, the first author, has calculated the odds of being murdered with a firearm in a number of advanced countries.[132] While one in every 29,000 Americans will be murdered with a gun each year, the odds are much lower in other countries: Israel = one in 95,000; Canada = one in 271,000; Australia = one in 655,000; and in Germany, the UK, and Japan, the odds of being murdered with a gun in any given year is less than one in a million. So much for the benefits of living in a country awash in guns.

Similarly, as seen in Chapter 3, states with higher levels of gun ownership tend to have more, not fewer, gun deaths, illustrating the fact that the presence of more guns makes places more dangerous. As shown in that chapter, nine of the ten states with the highest firearm mortality rates had gun ownership levels that exceeded national levels by about 20 percentage points. Thus, widespread gun ownership appears to lead to more deadly violence rather than serving as a deterrent to violence.

Homicide is the crime that is measured most accurately, because unlike with other types of crime, incidents are usually known to the police and more resources are spent by law enforcement to investigate suspected homicides. Killings are almost always reported to the police due to their gravity. In 2019, FBI data showed that there were 10,258 reported firearm homicides and just 334 justifiable homicides with firearms.[133] For every self-defense killing with a gun, there were thirty-one criminal homicides with guns, showing that guns are many times more likely to be used to commit murders than to kill in self-defense.

Another source, the Gun Violence Archive, shows that in 2021, there were 44,820 gun deaths in the United States, but just 1,237 verified defensive gun uses, or thirty-six gun deaths for every self-defense use of a gun.[134] This last figure does not even include all the nonfatal shootings that occur in the country every day. There are about twice the number of nonfatal as fatal shootings in the country each year;[135] therefore, the ratio of shootings (fatal and nonfatal) to self-defense gun uses is somewhere around 100:1. Consequently, gun-related deaths and injuries by aggressors outnumber defensive gun uses by a very large margin. When it comes to serious crimes and suicides with a gun, it is pure nonsense to suggest that guns are used more often for self-defense than to cause harm. It is not even close. Harmful gun uses occur far more frequently than beneficial, defensive ones.

The largest crime survey in the field of criminology is the US' National Crime Victimization Survey (NCVS). Each year, interviews are conducted with persons from about 150,000 households. A study of 14,000 personal "contact" crimes from the 2007-2011 surveys found that a gun was used in self-defense in fewer than 1 percent of the cases.[136] In addition, the use of a gun for protection, as opposed to some other protective action, did not diminish the chances that a victim would incur an injury. Overall, for the years 2007–2011, victims reported about half a million firearm-related victimizations a year and fewer than fifty thousand defensive gun uses per year—a ratio of ten criminal or aggressive gun uses to every defensive gun use.[137] A more recent analysis using NCVS data found that there are seven firearm victimizations for every defensive gun use.[138]

In one of the most influential studies in the gun violence field, physician Arthur Kellermann and his colleagues studied over 400 homicides occurring in residences in three counties.[139] They selected a control group by matching individuals who were not victims with the deceased on factors like neighborhood, race, sex, and age. After taking into account violence in the home, illegal drug use, and the presence of someone in the home with an arrest history, the researchers found that keeping a gun in the home was strongly and independently associated with a homicide in the home. Homes with guns were almost three times as likely to experience a homicide as homes without guns when other risk factors were statistically controlled.

Another study of homicide in the home led by Dr. Kellermann found that for every legally justifiable self-defense shooting with a gun kept in the home, there were twenty-two firearm-related assaults or murders, suicide attempts, or accidental shootings in or around the residence.[140] This study shows clearly that guns in the home are far more likely to harm members of the household than to be used against an intruder who would harm someone in that home.

A very large California study (of eighteen million adults living in the state) is in agreement with previous research.[141] Using the state's archive of firearm transactions, the researchers were able to identify handgun owners as well as those living with gun owners. They found that people living with handgun owners were twice as likely to die of a homicide than those in gun-free homes. People living with handgun owners were seven times more likely to be shot by their spouse or intimate partner. The study also showed that guns offered no protection from strangers, as those living with gun owners did not experience fewer homicides at the hands of strangers than those living in gun-free homes.

A survey of California adolescents probed hostile gun use against teens and self-defense gun use by adolescents.[142] Approximately 4 percent of the adolescents reported having been threatened with a gun at least once, while less than a third of 1 percent reported using a gun in self-defense. This translates to thirteen aggressive uses of a gun for every defensive use. In addition, most episodes of self-defense gun use appeared to be part of hostile interactions between adolescents with weapons, rather than the defensive use of a gun against someone who was a clear aggressor. The authors of this study concluded: "Far more California adolescents are threatened with a gun than use a gun in self-defense. Self-defense gun use is rare; many of the reported self-defense gun uses seem to be armed confrontations."[143]

Myth 14: There Are 2.5 Million Defensive Gun Uses Per Year in the US

Fact Check: Possibly the most outrageous claims on the use of guns for self-protection have been made by Gary Kleck and Mark Gertz, both formerly with Florida State University. Their study in the 1990s received much attention and has been referred to by many as proof that guns provide a net benefit to society. Kleck and Gertz based their conclusions on a national survey of less than 5,000 people, 222 of whom claimed one or more defensive gun uses over the previous year. The authors were left with 150 cases when they discarded those with incomplete or unreliable information. On the basis of these 150 survey respondents, the authors estimated that, each year, there are between 2.2 and 2.5 million uses of guns for the purpose of self-defense in the US.[144]

The reader should bear in mind that we have just presented evidence (in the previous section) from America's largest and most respected survey, the National Crime Victimization Survey (NCVS), which asks a representative sample of 240,000 persons from 150,000 households about crimes they have experienced over the previous year and the actions they have taken in relation to any victimizations.[145] As discussed, that survey showed that there are about fifty thousand defensive gun uses a year in the country. Thus, Kleck's and Gertz's finding of over two million defensive gun uses was more than forty times higher than those yielded by the NCVS.

Kleck's and Gertz's estimates for the entire population were based on the claims of just 150 people that they had used a gun in self-defense over the previous year. Perhaps the most significant error is in the interpretation of the claims by these respondents that their acts were really defensive rather than offensive. The authors acknowledged that they made no effort to assess whether the actions of respondents were truly defensive. In just a fifth of the cases did respondents indicate that they were actually attacked. Individuals claiming defensive gun uses indicated that the offender was armed with a gun in just 18 percent of the cases. In more than half the cases, the adversary had no weapon whatsoever. Thus, it is important to note that many claimed acts of self-defense were cases in which the respondent had not been attacked and most purported aggressors were unarmed. In some cases, a person claiming a defensive gun use merely referred to a gun rather than pointing or firing it.

Therefore, just a fraction of the 150 respondents in the original sample of close to 5,000 Americans reported a defensive gun use in which the adversary was armed and threatening or attacking the respondent and where the respondent actually wielded, pointed, or discharged the weapon.

Kleck and Gertz acknowledged that if only those cases are considered in which respondents believed their lives were in serious danger, their national estimates of defensive gun uses would range between 340,000 and 400,000. These numbers are less than a fifth of the 2.5 million defensive gun uses usually associated with this study. Even these numbers are seven to eight times the number yielded by the NCVS.

David Hemenway, director of Harvard University's Injury Control Research Center, has noted that Kleck's and Gertz's survey claimed that 845,000 defensive gun uses occurred during burglaries, a number exceeding the total number of burglaries occurring annually in the US in which residents owned a gun, were home, and were awake during a burglary.[146] Kleck's and Gertz's research would have us believe that more than 100 percent of all burglaries involved the defensive use of a gun by the home's occupant! In reality, an Atlanta study found that just 2 percent of cases in which a burglary occurred when someone was at home resulted in a defensive gun use.[147] Kleck and Gertz also estimated that about 200,000 offenders were shot by victims in one year, a number with little credibility as it was twice the total number of people who were treated for gunshot wounds in emergency rooms of American hospitals in that time.[148]

In short, both their own admitted shortcomings and the damning criticisms of leading researchers indicate that the Kleck and Gertz survey, which is often cited by gun rights advocates, has produced some highly inflated figures of defensive gun uses and has a serious credibility problem. A number of researchers nominate the Kleck and Gertz findings regarding defensive gun uses as "the most outrageous number mentioned in a policy discussion."[149]

Myth 15: Right-to-Carry Laws Reduce Crime

Fact Check: For more than thirty years, the National Rifle Association has aggressively promoted the view that carrying guns makes people safer. The term "constitutional carry" is one often used by those advocating for expanding the rights of gun owners. This cleverly coined term implies that the right of civilians to carry a gun on a daily basis is embedded in the Constitution—even though it is not—and that this right was with us in the early days of the American republic. In the 2008 US Supreme Court *Heller* ruling, Justice Antonin Scalia, writing for the majority, made it clear that prohibitions and restrictions relating to the carrying of firearms did not violate the Second Amendment.[150]

The regulation of gun carrying began in colonial times. Robert Spitzer of the State University of New York at Cortland argues that gun regulation was always a part of US history and that the current expansion of laws permitting gun carrying is foolhardy:

> We've learned this lesson before, in our own violent past, when strict regulation of concealed gun carrying was the near-universal and successful response to gun violence. As early as 1686, New Jersey enacted a law against wearing weapons because they induced "great Fear and Quarrels." Massachusetts followed in 1750. In the late 1700s, North Carolina and Virginia passed similar laws. In the 1800s, as interpersonal violence and gun carrying spread, 37 states joined the list. Tennessee's 1821 law fined "each and every person so degrading himself" by carrying weapons in public. Alabama's 1839 law was titled "An Act to Suppress the Evil Practice of Carrying Weapons Secretly." Why must we relearn a lesson we codified centuries ago? How dumb are we?[151]

The carrying of guns raises the possibility that spontaneous disputes and impulsive acts of violence may turn lethal. It also makes deadly errors more likely in active shooter situations as police can mistakenly believe that an armed civilian is a shooter. Consider an incident in Arvada, Colorado, in June, 2021. A "good Samaritan" credited with saving lives by intervening with an active shooter in Olde Town Arvada was shot and killed by a police officer.[152]

In another incident occurring on July 7, 2016, an individual opened fire and killed five Dallas police officers. The officers were on duty to provide security at a demonstration where the killing of African American men was being protested. About 20-30 open-carry activists were also on the scene, carrying assault weapons and wearing fatigues and body armor.

Police Chief Brown stated that the armed individuals impeded the law enforcement response by creating confusion as to who the shooter was and whether there were multiple shooters.[153] Brown stated: "We're trying as best we can as a law enforcement community to make it work so that citizens can express their Second Amendment rights," Brown said. "But it's increasingly challenging when people have AR-15s slung over their shoulder and they're in a crowd. We don't know who the good guy is versus the bad guy when everyone starts shooting."

On November 1, 2018, security guard Jemel Roberson stopped an active shooter in a Chicago bar and held the suspect at gunpoint until police arrived.[154] A responding white officer fatally shot Roberson, a twenty-six-year-old Black organist at a Chicago church, apparently thinking he was the shooter. Police Chief Dan Delaney later said, "Jemel Roberson was a brave man who was doing his best to end an active shooter situation at Manny's Blue Room."

The fatal shooting of Philando Castile is an example of the risks faced by Black concealed weapons permit holders. On July 7, 2016, two Minnesota police officers pulled over thirty-two-year-old Black motorist Philando Castile, whose partner and daughter were passengers in the car. Castile told the officers that he had a firearm and a license to carry. Still, officer Jeronimo Yanez fired seven shots and killed Castile when he reached for his identification.[155]

Starting in the late 1980s, US states began to weaken laws governing the carrying of concealed weapons. All states now allow gun carrying to some extent. A total of seventeen states have "shall issue" laws, which allow for little or no discretion in denying individuals a carry permit providing they meet basic requirements (e.g., applicants do not have a felony record).[156] Another twenty-five states require no permit nor training at all to carry a gun, and this number is growing. In just eight "may issue" states, the issuing authority has discretion to deny a permit if an applicant is deemed to lack "good character" or a good reason for carrying a gun in public. Most states also allow the open carrying of a handgun.

John Lott is an economist and an individual who has acknowledged assuming a false identity on the internet in order to praise his own work. A favorite of the gun lobby, Lott gave the concealed carry movement some credibility with the publication of his book *More Guns, Less Crime.* Lott's analyses covering 1985 to 1992 purported to show that states with *Shall Issue* laws experienced substantial declines in homicides, rapes, and aggravated assaults. Lott interpreted this finding to mean that offenders were deterred from committing crimes in places where they were more likely to encounter an armed victim.[157]

Lott's data have been reanalyzed, and his conclusions have been subject to harsh criticism by researchers from the public health, legal, public policy, and criminal justice fields. The National Research Council conducted an analysis with a time frame extended to the year 2000, and 17 of 18 panel members concluded that the existing research was inadequate to conclude that right-to-carry laws increased or reduced crime.[158] Further extending the analysis to 2010, John Donohue and his colleagues at Stanford University found that right-to-carry laws actually are "associated with substantially higher rates of aggravated assault, rape, robbery, and murder."[159] More recent analyses by Donohue and his colleagues show that state right-to-carry laws are associated with a 13–15 percent increase in violent crime ten years after the adoption of these laws.[160]

Dennis Henigan, formerly with the Brady Campaign to Prevent Gun Violence, pointed out that, in Lott's analysis, it was peculiar that the concealed carry laws showed the greatest effect in relation to crimes more often committed by intimates and acquaintances and showed little or no impact in relation to robbery, which is far more often a predatory crime involving strangers.[161] It is precisely in relation to crimes like robbery that the effect of gun carrying is expected to be greatest.

Philip Cook and Kristin Goss of Duke University added that those with permits to carry tend to be concentrated in rural and suburban areas where crime rates already are relatively low and where licensees are most often white, middle-aged, middle-class people who tend to have relatively low victimization rates.[162] Thus, the small proportion of individuals with permits, along with the lower-risk population that carries firearms, are unlikely to lead to more than a modest effect on crime rates.

David Fortunato of the University of California tested the idea of whether permissive concealed carry laws (*Shall Issue* laws) can deter people from committing crimes. In a national survey, he found that those in states with more permissive gun laws did not believe that more of their fellow residents carried a gun than those living in states with tougher, more restrictive gun laws.[163] Fortunato concluded that deterrence cannot happen if potential assailants in states with more permissive gun laws are not aware that more people are carrying.

A 2019 study by Paul Reeping of Columbia University and associates found that a ten-unit increase in the permissiveness of state gun laws, which includes right-to-carry laws, was associated with an 11.5 percent higher rate of mass shootings.[164] This study shows that lessening restrictions on guns and gun carrying affords no protection from mass shootings. In fact, weaker laws are associated with more mass shootings.

The ability of armed citizens to thwart shooters is also in doubt as a result of an FBI study of active shooter incidents over a twenty-year period.[165] A study of 333 such incidents, defined as one in which an individual is actively engaged in killing or attempting to kill people in a confined area, found that in just four (1 percent) of these incidents was a suspect killed by an armed civilian. Interviews with law enforcement officials in fifteen Michigan counties found that most of them could not cite a single defensive gun use in their jurisdiction in the previous twelve months. Furthermore, Louis Klarevas in his book, *Rampage Nation: Securing America from Mass Shootings*, has estimated that just one in every 1,876 actual or potential mass shootings is stopped by an armed civilian.[166]

The carrying of lethal weapons can also lead to escalation in the severity of disputes. The first author, in his 2021 book *CARNAGE: Preventing Mass Shootings in America*, found that ongoing or spontaneous disputes were the most common motives underlying mass shootings.[167] There also seems to be problems with the vetting of those granted a permit to carry firearms. Since May 2007, concealed carry permit holders have killed more than two thousand people and committed thirty-seven mass shootings, as well as many other crimes.[168]

One form of violence that has been surging is road rage shootings. The Gun Violence Archive has found that gun deaths and injuries in road rage incidents across the country increased by 98 percent from 2017 to 2021—a nearly 100 percent increase in less than five years. Such incidents cannot occur unless people carry firearms, and the carrying of guns is increasing in the US.[169]

More gun carrying is also leading to more thefts from cars. Thousands of guns are stolen from cars each year, and the numbers are skyrocketing. Groups of offenders steal guns for profit or for their criminal activity as they may be disqualified from purchasing guns, and stolen guns used in crimes cannot be traced back to them.[170]

Myth 16: The Training Required of Concealed Weapons Permit Holders Prepares Them for Effective Defensive Gun Use

Fact Check: All states now allow the carrying of concealed weapons, and most allow guns to be carried openly. An increasing number of states—twenty-five as this was being written—now allow the carrying of guns without a permit or any training at all.[171] This development, as well as laws passed in many states allowing people to carry guns into an increasing number of settings (e.g., college campuses, public meetings, courthouses, and airports) assume that people who carry guns know how to handle them safely and how to use them appropriately if the need arises. On the other hand, states with concealed weapon laws and firearms education and training are in fact saying that weapon carrying can pose a risk to public safety in the absence of some basic knowledge of the law and some degree of skill in the handling and use of firearms. How prepared are civilians for gun carrying and the use of guns for self-defense or in a combat situation?

One of the most exacting states is Delaware, which requires the expenditure of 100 rounds of ammunition and instruction on developing and maintaining shooting skills. This requirement is an acknowledgment of the need not just to acquire, but to maintain proficiency in shooting. Most states (thirty-one) do not even require that individuals seeking to carry guns undergo any amount of "live fire" training.[172] By contrast, police officers must maintain their skills on a regular basis.

Unlike other states, education and training in Delaware cover:

- Knowledge and safe handling of firearms and ammunition

- Safe storage of firearms and child safety

- Safe storage of ammunition and child safety

- Safe firearms shooting fundamentals

- Federal and state laws pertaining to the lawful purchase, ownership, transportation, use, and possession of firearms

- State laws pertaining to the use of deadly force for self-defense

- Techniques for avoiding a criminal attack and how to manage a violent confrontation, including conflict resolution[173]

Joseph Vince, an agent with the Bureau of Alcohol, Tobacco, Firearms and Explosives (ATF) for twenty-seven years and director of the criminal justice program at Mount St. Mary's University, is an internationally recognized expert on firearms and gun-related crime. Vince and his associates make the following observation on training:

> Since a firearm has immense lethality, the act of carrying one cannot be taken lightly. It should be given to those who have demonstrated good judgment, as well as mastered the necessary skills to handle this awesome responsibility. Legislators need to strengthen the vetting process of persons who are authorized to carry a firearm outside a residence. A simple criminal record check is not sufficient. Preventing criminal or accidental tragedies with firearms begins by allowing only those who have been properly trained initially and ongoing—and are known to be non-violent law-abiding citizens to carry in public. Likewise, no one who has anger, mental, or drug/alcohol issues should be permitted to carry a firearm. Certainly, an extensive law enforcement investigation of an applicant's background should be required to detect unsuitable candidates.[174]

Vince and his associates found that for a citizen to carry a firearm, training should include mental preparation, knowledge of the law, and development of situational judgment, as well as expertise, skill, and familiarity with firearms. They recommend basic initial training to receive a permit and biannual recertification to maintain the permit. Both basic and recertification training should consist of decision-making during real-life scenarios, shooting accuracy in stressful situations, and firing range practice.

The reality of how little training is required by states is frightening. Even states with mandatory training to obtain a permit to carry often have requirements that are very vague. For example, Florida, with two and a half million concealed weapons permit holders, does not specify the content of the courses permit holders must complete, only the qualifications necessary for instructors. There is no test for retention of the information covered about the law or the handling of a firearm, no test of marksmanship—a few shots are fired down the range, none of which need to hit a target—and no training with regard to judgment (when to shoot and when not to shoot), no recertification, just a renewal after seven years that can be done online. What passes as "training" in Florida is a single three-hour session, which includes time spent trying to sell students guns and insurance products.

Pete Blair, associate professor of criminal justice at Texas State University and director of the Advanced Law Enforcement Rapid Response Training Center, trains law enforcement personnel to respond to active shooter situations. He argues that real-world scenarios prepare police officers for high-stress situations. Blair notes that one would expect people without training to "freeze up or not know what to do, and to have difficulty performing actions correctly."[175]

David Chipman, a nominee to head the Bureau of Alcohol, Tobacco, Firearms, and Explosives (ATF) and a former agent with the ATF who spent several years on the agency's SWAT team, says, "Training for a potentially deadly encounter meant, at a minimum, qualifying four times a year throughout my twenty-five-year career. And this wasn't just shooting paper—it meant doing extensive tactical exercises. And when I was on the SWAT team, we had to undergo monthly tactical training."[176] Tactical officers receive training in when to hold their fire, and "blue-on-blue awareness," which reinforces the importance of considering whether other officers are present.

Research and police records show that even trained police officers miss their targets more often than they hit them during stressful combat situations. Greg Morrison, a former police officer and firearms instructor, states that there is some agreement among practitioners and researchers that in real-life crime situations, officers hit the mark once in every six shots.[177] Several analyses show that, in combat situations, trained officers miss the mark more than 80 percent of the time.

The civilian accuracy rate is much lower. Mike Weisser, a national gun expert, trainer, and author from Massachusetts, describes a drill[178] used in the training of many police officers—the Tueller drill:

> The drill requires an armed individual to pull, draw, point a pistol at a nine-inch diameter target which is 21 feet away and get off two shots within two seconds or less. Why 21 feet? Because most armed encounters take place in low light, and at 21 feet, an officer can usually determine if the person coming at him is also armed.

> Why 2 seconds? Because it takes a grown man roughly 2 seconds to run 21 feet. So...the Tueller drill allows the officer to demonstrate the proficiency which will make the difference between responding to an actual threat as opposed to gunning down an innocent man.

Weisser has conducted hundreds of these drills for law enforcement personnel. Typically, officers perform the two-shot drill ten times for a total of twenty shots. To be successful, they need to hit the target at least fifteen times. Just one or two officers in a hundred successfully perform the drill the first time. Weisser notes that after performing the drill six or seven times, muscle memory kicks in and officers hit the target fifteen or more times. By contrast, Weisser states that just 5 percent of his civilian students can successfully complete the Tueller drill after taking his safety course.[179] This result is with a stationary target and without the stress of a combat situation! Imagine the accuracy rate of civilians carrying guns in states requiring no permits or training whatsoever!

Weisser adds: "Know how many states require a Tueller drill in order to get a license to own a gun? None. Know how many states require a Tueller drill in order to get a license to walk around the neighborhood with a gun? None." Furthermore, Weisser states that many trainers lack any certification and that the gun industry is the only consumer product industry which has never developed a training certification process or even a definition of what is considered sufficient training in the use of a gun.

In addition to the above concerns about training, humans will sometimes misperceive threats; however, the presence of guns and a lack of training in assessing threats and the proper handling of firearms make fatal errors far more likely. Consider the following cases:

- A twenty-one-year-old Iowa woman was killed after she, along with her younger sister, tried to surprise her fiancé by hiding in a closet in his home. He heard a noise and saw the closet door open. When the girls jumped out of the closet, he fired and killed his fiancé with a handgun he kept for protection.[180]

- A seven-year-old boy was in critical condition after his grandmother mistook him for an intruder and shot him. She and her twin grandsons were sleeping after their father went to work. When she heard the bedroom door open, she assumed it was an intruder, grabbed the loaded revolver she kept by her bed, and fired one shot toward the door. As it turned out, she shot her grandson in the upper body.[181]

Joseph Vince and his colleagues underscore the importance of adequate training in light of what the typical attack on a civilian looks like:

> The average violent attack is over in 3 seconds. They are "blitz" attacks, designed to blindside and overwhelm us. We must be able to comprehend what's happening, orient ourselves to that attack, draw, and begin fighting back within that 3 second window, or else there's a very good chance we'll be defeated before we have a chance to even draw our weapons. The problem is, our bodies don't only choose between Fight and Flight, but instead between Fight, Flight, and Freeze. And without specific training, many (if not most) of us are prone to freezing for 3 or more seconds when confronted with a sudden, psychologically and physically overwhelming attack. We need training that will allow us to avoid violence whenever possible, but overcome, defeat, and survive violence when we can't avoid it.[182]

Myth 17: All Concealed Weapons Permit Holders Are "Good Guys"

We've seen in the preceding section that the state of training of those holding permits to carry guns throughout America is seriously inadequate and that training is actually nonexistent as a requirement to carry in half the states. What about the vetting of those carrying guns? In states where permits are required, is a careful screening conducted to ensure that individuals authorized to carry guns are, in fact, law-abiding citizens? This is the impression provided by gun rights advocates when bills are introduced to expand where gun owners can carry their firearms. The argument made is that only permit holders will be allowed to carry guns there, suggesting that these individuals are carefully vetted and pose no danger to the public.

Fact Check: In eight "may issue" states and the District of Columbia, the licensing authority is given wide discretion to deny an applicant a concealed carry permit if, for example, it is believed that the applicant lacks good character or a good reason to carry a firearm in public.[183] Another seven states allow limited discretion to deny permit applications where there is reasonable suspicion to believe that the applicant poses a danger to himself or others. The remainder of the states either lack a permitting requirement or may conduct a background check and require enrollment in a course prior to issuing a permit.

Simple background checks, which under federal law mean a search of several FBI databases, often fail to identify individuals who are irresponsible or display violent tendencies that have not yet led to a criminal conviction.[184] Many states fail to pass on juvenile history, mental health, and drug use records to the FBI. Disturbing social media posts, statements, and threatening behavior that does not result in a criminal conviction will not make their way into the FBI databases used to determine a person's suitability for gun ownership or a permit to carry guns. Thus, there is no factual basis to the idea that all permit holders are responsible people. In addition, people without criminal records can commit shootings in fits of jealousy and rage. Most killings arise out of a dispute, while a smaller number are felony killings.

Experience in Texas, Florida, and North Carolina illustrates that concealed weapons permit holders are not uniformly law-abiding. An analysis by the *Sun-Sentinel* newspaper in South Florida found that, in the first six months of 2006, 216 concealed carry permit holders had active arrest warrants, 128 individuals had domestic violence restraining orders against them, and 1,400 people pleaded guilty or no contest to felony charges.[185] Those receiving licenses to carry a gun included individuals convicted of manslaughter, aggravated assault, burglary, and sex crimes.

In first three years of Texas's concealed carry laws, those with permits were arrested for over 2,000 crimes, including homicide, kidnapping, rape, and other types of violent and property crimes.[186] A 2011 study by the *New York Times* in North Carolina found that over 2,400 permit holders were convicted of felonies or misdemeanors, excluding traffic-related crimes, over a five-year period. They included nearly 900 permit holders convicted of drunk driving and more than 200 convicted of weapons-related crimes. In about half of the more than 200 felony convictions, the holder's permit was not revoked or suspended, including in cases of murder and kidnapping. [187]

Furthermore, the Violence Policy Center (VPC) reported that during the first six months of 1997, the weapon-related arrest rate of concealed permit holders was more than twice that for the general adult population of Texas eligible to own handguns. A more recent report by the VPC has found that 2,015 people were murdered by concealed carry permit holders between May 2007 and September 2021.[188] Permit holders, including the shooter at the Orlando Pulse nightclub, were also responsible for thirty-seven mass shootings over this period.

The Violence Policy Center offers the following example of the brutal crimes concealed carry permit holders have committed and the inadequate vetting of individuals who apply for such permits:

On September 5, 2021, concealed handgun permit
holder Bryan Riley, 33, allegedly shot and killed Justice
Gleason, 40, [and] an unidentified 64-year-old woman, an
unidentified 33-year-old woman, and a three-month-old
boy during a shooting rampage at a home in Lakeland,
Florida. An 11-year-old girl was also wounded. Riley also
allegedly shot the family's dog. Sheriff's deputies, Lakeland
Police, SWAT, and other agencies responded to multiple
911 calls around 4:30 A.M. that morning about an active
shooter. According to a police report "deputies came under
attack" when they arrived on the scene. The Sheriff stated
that 100 rounds were fired between Riley, who was wearing
a bulletproof vest, and law enforcement. Riley was shot
once, but no deputies were wounded. Gleason and the
33-year-old female were found inside the home, with the
woman still holding the deceased infant. The 64-year-old
woman, believed to be the baby's grandmother, was found
in a separate home behind the first house. The 11-year-
old who was wounded said that she survived by playing
dead and praying. The Sheriff said the crime scene was
one of the worst he had ever seen and described Riley as
"evil in the flesh." After the shooting, Riley claimed he was
on meth and a survivalist. Riley's family said that he was
an honorably discharged Marine sharpshooter who [had]
served in Afghanistan and Iraq and suffered from PTSD.
Riley's girlfriend said that he had been acting erratically over
the past week after returning from his job as a security guard
at an Orlando church, claiming that he could talk directly
with God. Riley was charged with four counts of first degree
murder, one count of attempted first degree murder, and
seven counts of attempted first degree murder on a law
enforcement officer.[189]

Myth 18: Stand Your Ground Laws Save Lives

A majority of states have some version of a Stand Your Ground (SYG) law. The first of these laws was enacted in Florida in 2005. While they vary, these laws tend to give individuals the right to use deadly force when they have a "reasonable belief" that they are facing death or serious injury. Under these laws, no actual attack is necessary to justify the use of force, including lethal force. A person who has provoked someone or instigated a conflict and uses lethal force may still be granted immunity from prosecution if the person he has provoked responds violently to the provocation.

These laws represent a departure from the English tradition, which is the basis of laws in the colonies and then the United States.[190] Lawful self-defense usually required an attack by another person rather than simply a "reasonable belief" that an attack was imminent. In addition, English common law allowed for the use of lethal force when no other action was available that would allow the person to survive. Thus, traditionally, an individual who was able to "talk down" an attacker or leave the scene could not lawfully use lethal force to thwart the attacker. This is referred to as the "duty to retreat." Stand Your Ground laws also allow a person to use lethal force when there is a reasonable fear of death or serious bodily harm. There is no obligation under these laws to respond in a way that is less likely to cause death, but which is sufficient to repel the aggressor. This is why these laws are sometimes called "shoot first" laws.

Fact Check: A detailed *Tampa Bay Times* analysis of 200 Florida SYG cases found that, in nearly a third of the cases, defendants initiated the fight, shot an unarmed person, or pursued their victims—and still went free.[191] The *Tampa Bay Times* study showed that in 79 percent of the cases, the shooter could have retreated to avoid the confrontation.

Widespread gun carrying and a low level of firearms training in many states, along with SYG laws, combine to form a toxic brew. SYG legitimizes and enables the use of lethal violence, and widespread gun carrying ensures that many citizens have access to lethal weapons when disputes arise. SYG emboldens people to act like vigilantes rather than to solve disputes nonviolently, because they believe that a violent response is legitimate and that they will be immune from prosecution.

Justifiable homicides in Florida tripled following the introduction of SYG in 2005.[192] In 2016, the *American Medical Association's Internal Medicine Journal* published a study showing that Florida's SYG law was associated with a 24 percent increase in homicides and a 32 percent increase in firearm-related homicides.[193] It is estimated that an additional 4,200 people were murdered with a gun in Florida in the ten-year period following enactment of SYG.[194] Texas A&M researchers have found that homicide rates in twenty-one states with a SYG law increased by an average of 8 percent over other states, causing 600 more homicides per year in those states alone.[195] Furthermore, this study found that SYG laws did *not* deter crimes such as robbery and aggravated assault.

SYG laws also have disturbing side effects. John Roman, a Senior Fellow at the Urban Institute, analyzed data from the FBI Supplemental Homicide Reports to conduct a comparative analysis of justified homicide rates from 2005 to 2010 in SYG and non-SYG states. Although racial disparities are also found in states without SYG laws, these disparities were significantly greater in SYG states. In these states, a white shooter who killed a Black victim was 350 percent more likely to be found to be justified in the killing than if the same shooter killed a white victim.[196] In these states, justifiable shooting rulings ranged from 3 percent to 15 percent for white-on-white, Black-on-white, and Black-on-Black killings. When the shooter was white and the victim Black, 36 percent of homicides were ruled justified.

It has been estimated that approximately thirty to fifty people a month are killed in the US as a result of SYG laws.[197] Overall, the evidence shows that SYG laws increase homicide rates and do not act as a deterrent to crime. They have also been found to be applied inequitably depending on the race of the shooter and victim.

Myth 19: Most Mass Shootings Occur in Gun-Free Zones

Following the Columbine High School mass shooting in 1999, NRA Executive Vice President Wayne LaPierre stated: "First, we believe in absolutely gun-free, zero-tolerance, totally safe schools. That means no guns in America's schools, period...with the rare exception of law enforcement officers or trained security personnel."[198]

However, the NRA's position changed following the massacre at Sandy Hook Elementary School in 2012 when LaPierre took the position that the only defense against a shooter was "a good guy with a gun." This position became a mantra for gun rights advocates, who began to attribute mass shootings in certain settings (including schools and airports) to policies forbidding people from bringing guns into those settings. The argument is that "gun-free" zones are magnets for mass shooters. It is claimed that these shooters select gun-free zones because they know they will succeed where there are no armed civilians to stop them.

Researcher John Lott claimed that 98 percent of mass shootings from 1950 to the present occurred in gun-free zones.[199] He claimed that mass shooters target such areas because they know they will not face armed resistance. Therefore, to Lott, the way to stop mass shootings is to ensure that civilians are able to carry firearms in as many places as possible.

Fact Check: The problem with the above line of argument is that many settings prohibiting civilian gun carrying (such as colleges and football stadiums) have armed security officers. Thus, even where gun carrying by civilians is banned, armed officers are frequently present. In America, few large venues are truly gun free. Louis Klarevas of Columbia University found that just 13 out of 111 high-fatality mass shootings (12 percent) occurring between 1966 and 2015 occurred in true gun-free zones with no armed security or armed civilians, and just 5 percent occurred in a zone in which civilian gun carrying alone was banned.[200] Security personnel and/or armed civilians were in a position to engage shooters in almost nine out of ten mass shootings. Despite this fact, the shooters proceeded with their attack.

According to an FBI study of active shooter incidents, nearly two-thirds of the shooters committed suicide or were shot and either killed or wounded by the police or others, indicating that these shootings are high-risk undertakings.[201] Thus, the notion that arming even more people in a variety of settings will serve as a deterrent is questionable, given the risks many mass shooters are prepared to face, often including their own self-destructive behavior. The concept of deterrence is based on a rational actor who seeks to avoid harm, whereas many of these people are on suicide missions.

John Lott's claim that 98 percent of mass shootings occur in gun-free zones is fraught with errors. For the period 1977–1997, Lott counted each individual death in mass shootings as an entire mass shooting. Lott's own calculations indicated that fourteen mass shootings occurred in Oklahoma in 1986. There was just one mass shooting (defined as four or more people killed) in that year in which fourteen people were killed (excluding the shooter). Errors of this type exaggerated the number of mass shootings between 1977 and 1997 and had the effect of increasing Lott's calculated percentage of mass shootings that occurred in gun-free zones. Lott also misclassified shootings, sometimes failed to adhere to his own definition of such shootings, and omitted large-scale shootings.[202]

In *CARNAGE: Preventing Mass Shootings in America*, the first author, Tom Gabor, examined 1,029 mass shootings occurring in the US in 2019 and 2020. Seven in ten took place on the street, in or around a residence, or in or around a bar or club.[203] With the exception of bars and restaurants serving alcohol, which are subject to prohibitions on gun carrying in about half the states, the most common locations of mass shootings are those in which civilian gun carrying is usually allowed. Streets, residences, most businesses, private vehicles, parks, apartment complex grounds, and parking lots are all places that tend not to be subject to federal or state prohibitions. Therefore, the results of this study are consistent with previous research showing that the overwhelming majority of mass shootings do not occur in true "gun-free" zones.

The reality is that mass shootings are happening in schools, public spaces, places of worship, and business worksites that do include armed law enforcement. The recent shootings in a Buffalo shopping center and in Highland Park, Illinois, were only the latest examples. As noted in Chapter 3, armed law enforcement officers were on scene during the Parkland and Uvalde shootings as well. A determined shooter with the means to acquire weapons and ammunition will be undeterred, and the consequences of our failure to address ease of access to these weapons and the social conditions underlying the violence will continue to cost many lives.

Guns and Self-Defense: The Bottom Line

- If guns provided a net benefit to society, the US, which has the largest armed civilian population in the world, ought to be among the safest nations in the world. Instead, this country has twenty-five times the gun homicide rate of other high-income countries. States with higher levels of gun ownership tend to have more, not fewer, gun deaths, illustrating the fact that more guns make places more dangerous. FBI data show that, for every self-defense killing with a gun, there are thirty-one criminal homicides with guns. A study of homicide in the home found that for every legally justifiable self-defense shooting with a gun kept in the home, there were twenty-two firearm-related assaults or murders, suicide attempts, or accidental shootings in or around the residence. This study shows clearly that guns in the home are far more likely to harm members of the household than to be used against an intruder who would harm someone in that home.

- Defensive gun uses probably number around 50,000 per year in the United States, an estimate arrived at by the very large and highly respected National Crime Victimization Survey. The 2.5 million "mythical number" suggested by researchers Gary Kleck and Mark Gertz is highly inflated by their own admissions as to the limitations of their study. Other researchers have shown that the 2.5 million figure lacks credibility. Taking the number of 50,000 annual defensive gun uses, the number of criminal uses of guns far exceeds defensive uses by a ratio of at least 10:1.

- Right-to-carry laws appear to increase, not reduce, rates of gun violence. Incidents in which armed civilians thwart active shooters are rare. In addition, these laws produce a number of side effects. More widespread gun carrying leads to more incidents in which spontaneous altercations escalate to lethal violence or serious bodily injury. The practice of open carry can confuse law enforcement when they are responding to an active shooter incident. More gun carrying leads to more thefts of guns from cars, which, in turn, make more guns available for criminal use.

- The majority of states either lack any training requirement for those who will carry guns or have set requirements well below what is recommended by leading experts. Even with the most rigorous training, the effective use of firearms for self-defense is a challenge since attacks tend to occur by surprise and the victim has little time to react. When training is inadequate, deadly mistakes and other harmful uses of firearms are likely to outnumber defensive uses by a wide margin.

- The process for vetting and training of individuals who lawfully carry firearms is not rigorous in most states. Apart from conducting basic background checks, most states do not ensure that individuals who are licensed to carry are of good character, and required training in the use of firearms tends to be very cursory. Carrying also has its inherent risks since spontaneous disputes do arise, and the presence of guns at these times can lead to dangerous escalation. The number of concealed weapons license holders who have been involved in serious crimes provides further evidence that individuals carrying guns can pose a risk to public safety. Because much violence arises spontaneously, it may be the case that there are no true "good guys," as many people are capable of violence if they feel threatened or are sufficiently angry. With the addition of a loaded gun, a lethal outcome is more likely.

- While they vary, Stand Your Ground laws tend to give individuals the right to use deadly force when they have a "reasonable belief" that they are facing death or serious injury. Under these laws, no actual attack is necessary to justify the use of force, including lethal force. Unlike self-defense laws in the past, there is no duty to retreat in a dispute with these statutes. SYG emboldens people to act like vigilantes rather than to solve disputes nonviolently because they believe that a violent response is legitimate and that they will be immune from prosecution. SYG laws have tended to increase the number of homicides in states where they have been implemented and have not been found to deter violent crimes. There are also major racial disparities in their implementation because a white shooter killing a Black person is far more likely to have their actions deemed to be justified than shooters in cases involving a Black shooter or a white victim.

- True gun-free zones account for about one in ten mass shootings. In nearly two-thirds of active shooter incidents, the shooter committed suicide or was shot (and either killed or wounded) by police or security personnel. Such shootings are therefore high-risk endeavors for shooters, indicating that many are indifferent to the risks they face. As a result, arming more individuals in these settings is not likely to deter such perpetrators.

Chapter 6

THE TRUTH ABOUT THE CAUSES OF GUN VIOLENCE

Myth 20: The US Has More Gun Deaths Than Other Countries Because It Is More Violent and Not Due to Higher Gun Ownership or Weaker Gun Laws

It is often argued that it is not our high level of gun ownership that is responsible for the high rate of gun deaths in the US relative to other advanced countries. Rather, the argument goes, the US is simply more prone to crime and violence. Guns are merely brought along when people commit crimes that would have occurred even in their absence.

Fact Check: The evidence does not support this position. The International Crime Victims Survey of 2004–2005 compared the extent of criminal victimization in thirty countries, including the US, Canada, Mexico, Australia, New Zealand, many European countries, and several Asian, African, and Latin American countries. National surveys were conducted in each country, and respondents answered a series of questions on criminal victimizations they had experienced over the previous year.[204] Overall, the US ranked somewhere in the middle in terms of crime overall, just above average for car theft, burglary, theft of personal property, assaults, and threats and below average for robbery. Sexual assault was the one offense in which the US ranked high relative to other countries. The International Crime Victims Survey of 2000 found that for eleven crimes (excluding homicide) the US had an overall victimization rate that was slightly below the median for seventeen other industrialized nations.[205] Therefore, the much higher levels of lethal violence and firearm homicide in the US cannot be explained by a general tendency of Americans to commit more criminal acts or to be more violent than citizens of other developed nations.

It is in relation to homicide, especially gun homicide, that the US stands apart when compared with other high-income countries. In their seminal book *Crime Is Not the Problem: Lethal Violence in America*, legal scholars Franklin Zimring and Gordon Hawkins have shown that the US does not in fact stand out as more violent or crime-prone relative to other advanced countries.[206] Where it stands out is in its levels of lethal violence. Zimring and Hawkins show that burglary and theft rates in the US are comparable to those in other developed Western countries. The US has about the same level of ordinary crimes as many other nations. In fact, people living in Australia, New Zealand, and Canada are more likely to be victims of assault.

However, when it comes to lethal violence, the US stands alone with a rate of criminal homicide that is many times that of most affluent countries. Zimring and Hawkins state that American violence is so dangerous due to the widespread availability of guns: "Firearms use is so prominently associated with the high death rate from violence that starting with any other topic would rightly be characterized as an intentional evasion."[207] Zimring and Hawkins note that close to a third of American homicides arise from arguments rather than crimes. Gun possession and use is an obvious reason why arguments in America turn deadly since the majority of homicides involve guns. Guns are used in 4 percent of all major crimes, 20 percent of all violent crimes, and 70 percent of all homicides, illustrating the association between gun use and homicide.

While the US has 3.7 times the *non-gun* murder rate of England and Wales, it has 63 times the *gun* murder rate of these countries, resulting in an overall murder rate (gun and non-gun) that is 8.5 times that of England and Wales. This situation demonstrates the extent to which the gap in homicides between the US and England/Wales is elevated by the frequent presence of guns in the US when disputes occur. When guns are taken out of the equation and we look at homicides without guns, the difference between the US and other countries is far less dramatic, illustrating that the cultural argument does not account for America's outlier status in relation to homicide overall.

Along similar lines, the argument has been made that the US has more gun violence than other advanced countries due to a greater appetite for violent video games and violent media content. In fact, this is not the case; in Japan, South Korea, and the UK, all of which have only a fraction of America's gun violence deaths relative to their population, residents spend more per capita on violent video games than do Americans.[208]

Myth 21: Mass Shootings and Gun Violence Are Primarily Due to the Mental Illness of the Perpetrator

This belief has been expressed frequently by the gun lobby following massacres. After the murder of twenty-six congregants and the wounding of another twenty in a church in Sutherland Springs, Texas, President Trump completely adopted this position, calling the shooting a mental health problem, not a "guns situation." The implication of labeling mass murders as a mental health issue is that changes in gun laws are avoided and social conditions underlying violence are not addressed.

Fact Check: Mental illness is not a useful predictor of future violent behavior, as those so afflicted are not any more likely than the average person to carry out a shooting or other violent act unless they possess other high-risk factors, such as substance abuse. The mentally ill do have an elevated likelihood of committing suicide. About 4 percent of violent acts are committed by a mentally ill person.[209]

A study of 133 mass shootings has shown that these incidents often have a domestic violence link, while in just 11 percent of the incidents had concerns about the mental health of the shooter been brought to the attention of a medical practitioner, legal authority, or school official.[210] That study also showed that when assault weapons or high-capacity magazines were used, an average of eight more people were shot, indicating the pivotal role of the weapon in increasing the carnage. The call to address the nation's mental health issues is a familiar dodge of those seeking to avoid a discussion of gun policy.

The US has 5 percent of the world's population, but over a third of all mass shootings.[211] While in the top tier of comparison countries, American rates of mental illness are not out of line with those of other countries.[212] Any differences in the prevalence of mental illness fail to account for the enormous gap in the number of mass shootings between the US and other advanced nations. Countries such as the UK, Germany, and Japan have at most a few dozen gun homicides, and no more than one or two mass shootings per year. By contrast, the US has had over 600 mass shootings each year in 2020 and 2021.[213] Therefore, the gap in mass shootings is too great to be explained by more modest differences in the rates of mental illness.

Psychiatrist Richard Friedman writes that psychiatry cannot protect us from mass murderers.[214] He states that while many mass shooters have a severe personality or psychotic disorder, they often avoid the mental health system altogether because they are not interested in treatment and do not see themselves as ill. He adds that it is difficult, if not impossible, to predict which individuals will become violent. While millions of Americans have a mental disorder or a serious anger management issue, just an infinitesimal fraction of them will commit these atrocities. Friedman argues that the focus should not be on detecting mass killers in advance, but on the availability of lethal weapons. He points to Australia, a country that has virtually eliminated mass shootings since automatic and semiautomatic long guns were banned.

Dr. Michael Stone, a forensic psychiatrist at Columbia University, maintains a database of about 350 mass killers over one century.[215] He notes that 65 percent exhibited no signs of a severe mental disorder. About 22 percent were psychotic, compared to 1 percent of the population. The majority were not mentally ill but disgruntled workers and jilted lovers with a deep sense of injustice. Most experience long-term stress due to failure at school, work, and/or relationships, blame others, and the stress builds. Then, one final life stressor can set them off. About 40 percent had substance abuse problems.

J. Reid Meloy, a forensic psychologist, believes that many mass shooters fall along a "paranoid spectrum." At the extreme end is full-on psychosis, but the majority of people on this spectrum are not deeply ill. Rather, they accumulate injustices and often blame them on one person or one group. There is an intense urge to stop the perceived persecution. The person may never act on the urge, but, if they do, there is a triggering event, such as a loss in love or work.

In the book *CARNAGE*, Tom Gabor studied over one thousand mass shootings (four or more people shot in the same general location, excluding the shooter) in 2019–2020. He found that in just eleven of the cases was there a clear indication of mental illness or instability. Many cases were not solved, so there were undoubtedly more involving mental illness. This said, the largest categories of mass shootings involved disputes, either ongoing or spontaneous, that culminated in a shooting at a party, bar, or on the street.[216]

Underlying many mass shootings that appear senseless and that are fueled by conflicts is a sense of hopelessness rather than mental illness. Gabor was struck by the large number of urban mass shootings committed in crowds in which the shooter(s) displayed utter recklessness. Often young children were shot. These were not shootings where an individual had planned over weeks or months to kill a maximum number of individuals. Rather, these shootings often involved small groups engaged in a cycle of retaliatory shootings.

Interviews with at-risk youth in some of New York City's toughest neighborhoods were very revealing with regard to the connection between gun violence, hopelessness, and despair. Codes of conduct promoting violence also can develop in communities where status is hard to achieve through conventional work. Youth interviewed in New York noted that economic stresses on them and their families led them to commit robberies and engage in drug dealing and confirmed that these activities required guns.[217] They didn't romanticize their actions. As one youth said: " 'Cause when you broke, you get angry about everything, and then you grab your gun and just do robberies and do stuff you not supposed to be doing to get your money."

Some of the youth carried guns because of their belief that they could face retaliation or other dangers at any time. Some mentioned a fear of the police. Said a twenty-four-year-old man: "You gotta protect your life because the cops might shoot you." A twenty-one-year-old said gun carrying was a matter of self-preservation: "I got to keep my gun. Cops want to kill me. Dudes want to kill me. I don't know if I'll be alive tomorrow." Another youth mentioned the code that requires an individual to retaliate if their friends are hurt: "I have to carry one [a gun]. I got beefs. They shoot at my friends. So I have to shoot back."

Some of the youth reported they felt powerful with a gun. They also explained that being territorial in defending their neighborhood gave them a sense of ownership over their home turf even though actual home ownership was unlikely; "We shoot each other over land that is not ours. It's feeling that you want to have something. We don't own a house. We don't pay the rent. But this is my block, and you can't come here."

Gabor's analysis in *CARNAGE* found that the data supported many of these statements on the street. Rather than mental illness, economic conditions in which opportunities to earn a decent living are severely limited can create a sense of hopelessness and can lead men to believe that material needs and status can best be achieved through crime and membership in a gang or crew. An analysis of American cities shows that rates of gun homicide and mass shootings are higher in cities where a higher proportion of the population lives in a distressed neighborhood. A distressed neighborhood is not only one in which many residents are poor or out of work; such communities also have few business start-ups, a less educated population, and more vacant properties. These conditions foster a sense of hopelessness. For example, Detroit, Memphis, and Baltimore, where over half the residents live in distressed zip codes, had much higher homicide rates than cities like New York and Los Angeles, where less than 20 percent of the population live in a distressed area.[218]

After sitting through much of the criminal trial for the Parkland shooter, author Fred Guttenberg was left asking whether it matters if we don't do anything about mental illness. If we don't do anything to make it harder for those with potential risk factors for violence to acquire the means to do so, does it matter? The reality is that the majority of those with mental illness who use a gun for violence are using it on themselves. Simply blaming mental illness won't stop that. For any determined killer, with or without mental illness, if we do nothing to address the easy acquisition of guns and ammunition, it won't matter. It is just another empty and meaningless slogan by the gun lobby and gun extremists to blame others while ensuring we do nothing to address the real causes of gun violence.

Causes of Gun Violence: The Bottom Line

- An international survey and other sources show that the US has an overall crime victimization rate that ranks somewhere in the middle when compared with other industrialized countries. Therefore, higher gun death rates in the US cannot be due to higher levels of crime and violence overall. This finding suggests that the higher level of gun ownership in the US is likely a critical factor in explaining higher American gun death rates. In addition, comparisons with other countries, like the UK, show a much wider gap in the gun versus non-gun homicide rate, showing that the greater availability of guns in the US widens the overall gap in homicide rates.

  What factor other than gun availability could explain the fact that the US has about 60 times the gun murder rate of England and Wales, but only four times the non-gun murder rate of these two countries?[219] Legal scholars Zimring and Hawkins point out that many homicides in the US arise from arguments and that the presence of guns in so many of these encounters accounts for much of the difference in lethal violence between the US and other countries.

- Most violent acts, including mass shootings, are not committed by individuals with serious mental illnesses. While some acts are committed by the mentally ill, blaming mass shootings on mental illness is a diversion from the role of weapons and socioeconomic conditions. The US has levels of mental illness that are comparable to other countries, but its levels of mass shootings are far in excess of most nations. Psychiatrists note that the majority of shooters are individuals with repeated failures at school, work, or relationships who blame others and may be set off by one final major stressor. Psychiatrists indicate they cannot predict who the next shooter will be among millions who are *potentially* prone to violence; therefore, many argue that tackling the availability of lethal weapons is the best way to prevent these shootings.

A study by the first author has found that the most frequent features of mass shootings are disputes involving individuals or small groups, either ongoing or spontaneous in origin. The presence of highly lethal weapons enables mass shootings, including the shooting of innocent bystanders. A disproportionate amount of violence, including gun violence, occurs in highly distressed neighborhoods characterized by high levels of poverty, low educational achievement, and other conditions that limit the ability of residents to live a productive life. Hypermasculinity codes may flourish in these neighborhoods as violence may be a way of achieving status as well as economic goals.

Chapter 7

THE TRUTH ABOUT GUNS AND THE CONSTITUTION

Myth 22: The Second Amendment Grants Americans the Right to Carry Any Firearm into Any Setting

The Second Amendment to the US Constitution reads: "A well regulated Militia, being necessary to the security of a free State, the right of the people to keep and bear Arms shall not be infringed." A segment of American gun owners believes that the much debated "right to keep and bear arms" afforded by the Second Amendment is absolute and therefore any limits on owners' rights is a violation of the Constitution. Thus, these Americans believe that people can bring any gun anywhere for any purpose.

Fact Check: First, no rights are absolute. For example, freedom of speech, guaranteed by the First Amendment, does not mean you can threaten, defame, incite, pass on national secrets, encourage people to commit suicide, or yell "Fire!" in a crowded theater knowing there is no fire.

During World War I, Charles Schenck and Elizabeth Baer passed out
leaflets stating that the military draft violated the Thirteenth Amendment
prohibition against involuntary servitude. The leaflets urged people
to disobey the draft. Schenck and Baer were charged and convicted
with conspiracy to violate the Espionage Act of 1917 by encouraging
insubordination in the military and obstructing recruitment. Their
defense was that they were exercising their First Amendment right of free
speech. In their appeal, the US Supreme Court held that the Espionage
Act did not violate the First Amendment and Justice Oliver Wendell
Holmes wrote that the First Amendment did not protect speech that
presents a danger of a significant evil that Congress has the power
to prevent.[220]

There are no rights without limits, because exercising our personal
liberties may harm others and encroach on their rights or those of
the community. If an individual decides to fire a gun at a target in his
suburban backyard, he may annoy, frighten, or harm his neighbors.
Carrying a gun into an airport or college campus may intimidate, harm,
or interfere with another person's ability to travel safely or study in a safe
environment. Living in a society with others means balancing rights.

America's first Constitution, the Articles of Confederation (1778),
required that each state maintain a well-regulated and disciplined
militia in the event of a war.[221] There was no official military force in
the US until 1789. Michael Waldman, a constitutional lawyer with the
Brennan Center for Justice, has argued that the framers of the current
Constitution did not consider the rights of individuals to guns outside of
militia service at all when they were drafting the Second Amendment. In
his book, *The Second Amendment: A Biography*, Waldman wrote that the
notes of James Madison and the other framers from the Constitutional
Convention of 1787 did not mention private gun ownership, guns for
self-defense, or guns for hunting.[222]

Throughout most of America's history, the courts have not viewed the Second Amendment as protecting individual gun rights at all. For 200 years, the right to keep and bear arms was viewed as a collective right. From 1876–2001, forty-one decisions by the US Supreme Court and Courts of Appeal have consistently set aside challenges to gun laws and have seen the Second Amendment as protecting state militias rather than individual rights. Four times between 1876 and 1939, the US Supreme Court declined to rule that the Second Amendment protected individual gun ownership outside the context of a militia.[223] In his influential work on the Constitution, Associate Justice of the Supreme Court Joseph Story took the view that the Second Amendment referred to militias and wrote the following: "The militia is the natural defense of a free country against sudden foreign invasions, domestic insurrections, and domestic usurpations of power by rulers."[224] Saul Cornell, a leading historian specializing in early American and Constitutional history, has argued that the amendment was conceived to allow Americans to fulfill their civic obligation to form militias.[225]

Every single article on the Second Amendment published in a law review between 1888 and 1959 concluded it did not guarantee an individual the right to a gun.[226] From the late 1970s, a number of attorneys and professors, including many funded by the NRA, began to turn out a large volume of articles making the case that the Second Amendment did protect the right of individuals to own guns. Public opinion shifted and, by 2008, 73 percent of Americans believed the Second Amendment "guaranteed the rights of Americans to own guns" outside a militia.

The 2008 *Heller* decision, the conservative-majority US Supreme Court's influential and most pro-gun rights ruling to that point, established for the first time an individual's right to gun ownership in the home for self-defense. However, the Court made it clear that this right was not extended to everyone (felons and the mentally ill are generally prohibited from gun ownership), or to every venue (since guns can be excluded from sensitive settings like schools), or to all types of firearms ("dangerous and unusual weapons" can be prohibited). The Court asserted that limits imposed on gun ownership were in conformity with the US Constitution's Second Amendment.

Writing for the majority, Justice Antonin Scalia, a gun owner himself, stated:

> Like most rights, the Second Amendment right is not unlimited. It is not a right to keep and carry any weapon whatsoever in any manner whatsoever and for whatever purpose: For example, concealed weapons prohibitions have been upheld under the Amendment or state analogues. The Court's opinion should not be taken to cast doubt on longstanding prohibitions on the possession of firearms by felons and the mentally ill, or laws forbidding the carrying of firearms in sensitive places such as schools and government buildings, or laws imposing conditions and qualifications on the commercial sale of arms. Miller's holding that the sorts of weapons protected are those "in common use at the time" finds support in the historical tradition of prohibiting the carrying of dangerous and unusual weapons.[227]

Those of us who write opinion pieces in the newspapers or online often receive very angry comments from individuals who believe that any restriction on gun ownership is contrary to the Constitution. Their views stem from a lack of knowledge of the history of higher court decisions and are based on highly selective, second-hand knowledge of the Heller decision. Many probably rely on highly biased information sources that aim to promote the gun rights position rather than inform readers accurately about what is contained in the 157-page decision. Everyone with internet access can read the actual, unfiltered version of the Heller decision on the Supreme Court's website: www.supremecourt.gov/opinions/07pdf/07-290.pdf.

A decision of the US Supreme Court in June 2022 (*Bruen* ruling) further departed from two hundred years of precedent by taking the view that the Second Amendment protects a right to carry guns outside the home for self-defense.[228] The Court ruled that New York State violated the right to keep and bear arms for self-defense by requiring them to show they had a special need for self-protection in order to obtain a permit to carry a firearm. The Court noted that the right to carry a firearm was deeply rooted in American history. However, as shown in Chapter 2, firearm regulations are also deeply rooted in US history. This said, the majority opinion acknowledged that restrictions on firearms in sensitive places may be appropriate and that many state restrictions, such as background checks, firearms training, and mental health record checks, were still permissible.

The Second Amendment right is therefore a limited right. While much has been said and written about the Second Amendment and the extent to which it protects gun rights, little has been written about the responsibility of federal and state governments to protect their populations from unrelenting attacks on the lives and liberties of citizens by individuals wielding guns. To present a balanced picture of rights relating to guns, we need to ask the following questions:

Do Americans have the right to be safe in their communities? Do children have the right to attend school without the constant threat of a mass shooting? Do people have the right to express themselves on controversial issues at public rallies and in educational institutions without the fear of being shot? Do Americans have the right to worship and participate in leisure activities without being shot?"

America's founding documents and commitments under international law suggest that the answer to these questions is an unequivocal yes. No discussion of rights related to guns is complete without acknowledging the public's right to be protected from gun violence. Consider the following:

- In the Declaration of Independence, America's founders stated that the right to Life, Liberty, and the pursuit of Happiness were inalienable rights. Therefore, these rights cannot be forfeited. Attorney Jonathan Lowy, one of America's most active litigators in cases involving guns, has written:

  "America's First Freedom" is not the right to firearms; it is the freedom that the founders, in fact, announced first: the right to life, liberty, and the pursuit of happiness. The right to life—or to live—is protected by the Constitution and is the bedrock principle on which our government and civil society are founded... Courts have recognized that public safety (which derives from, and is intended to protect, that right) is paramount, and no rights may expose people to the risk of imminent harm.[229]

- The right to life is protected by the Constitution. The Fifth Amendment includes the following protections: "...nor shall any person...be deprived of life, liberty or property, without due process of law." The Fourteenth Amendment includes the following protections: "...nor shall any State deprive any person of life, liberty, or property, without due process of law."

- The Preamble to the Constitution referred to "domestic tranquility." Here the Founding Fathers expressly imposed a duty on the federal government to protect the safety and security of citizens.[230]

- The US has signed or ratified numerous international agreements, including the Universal Declaration of Human Rights, which affirms that "Everyone has the right to life, liberty, and security of the person (Article 3)."[231] The International Covenant on Civil and Political Rights states that no person "shall be arbitrarily deprived of his life" (Article 6).[232]

- Amnesty International has condemned the US for breaching commitments under international law by failing to enact gun laws to protect its population. Amnesty argues in a 2018 report, *In the Line of Fire*, that the US has breached its commitments under international human rights law: "The USA has failed to implement a comprehensive, uniform and coordinated system of gun safety laws and regulations, particularly in light of the large number of firearms in circulation, which perpetuates unrelenting and potentially avoidable violence, leaving individuals susceptible to injury and death from firearms."[233]

- Amnesty further notes that, as part of the right to life and other human rights, the responsibility of nations to prevent gun violence requires: (1) restricting access to firearms, especially on the part of those at an elevated risk of misusing them; and (2) implementing violence reduction measures where misuse of firearms persists. The human rights group asserts that nations "should establish robust regulatory systems," including licensing, registration, restriction of certain weapon types, safe storage, research, and policy development. Nationally, the US has done little or nothing in relation to any of these policies for more than twenty-five years, and, due to the influence of the gun lobby, has seen Congress suppress funding for research on gun violence since 1996. Amnesty notes that countries not only have obligations to protect the lives of individuals from state agents but from actual or foreseeable threats at the hands of private individuals as well.

Violence is especially foreseeable in low-income neighborhoods with persistently high levels of violence, poor public services, and policing that may not comply with international standards.

- The oldest justification for government is the protection of citizens, and this purpose requires that taxes be collected to support an army and police force, to maintain courts and jails, and to elect or appoint officials responsible for implementing laws.[234] Sir Edward Coke, a seventeenth century English jurist, wrote of the concept of a contract between the King and his subjects according to which the latter obey and the King protects. Philosopher John Locke then built on this concept of a social contract, basing it instead on the democratic will of a free people entering into society with each other and establishing a government for the preservation of their natural rights. Individuals come together to form a community to preserve their lives, liberties, and property. These individuals agree to give up their power to act for their own preservation and to be regulated by the laws of the society. Each individual also cooperates with others to assist "the Executive Power of the society" as required by law. In return, citizens receive the benefits, assistance, and protection of the community. According to Locke, the role of government is to secure life, liberty, and property. When it fails to accomplish this, "[It] is dissolved, and the community gains the right to form a new form of government."

In the eighteenth century, the English jurist (judge) Sir William Blackstone asserted that society is an association for mutual protection whereby an individual contributes to the economic subsistence and peace of the society, helping enforce laws and defending the community against rebellion or invasion, and then receives protection from the community. Personal security, personal liberty, and private property were viewed as absolute rights, originating in the state of nature. Following the Civil War, members of the 39th Congress asserted the notion that citizens had the right to protection by their government, and that, in return, citizens offered their obedience. "Protection and allegiance are reciprocal....It is the duty of the Government to protect; of the subject to obey," said Senator Alvin Stewart of Nevada. Senator Justin Morrill of Vermont chimed in: "These are the essential elements of citizenship...allegiance on one side and protection on the other."

- A number of the original state constitutions in the United States adopted the view that society was founded on a contract and affirmed the right to life, protection, and security. Right up to the present day, the Massachusetts Constitution explicitly refers to a social contract in its preamble: "The body politic is formed by a voluntary association of individuals: it is a social compact, by which the whole people covenants with each citizen, and each citizen with the whole people, that all shall be governed by certain laws for the common good." Another example is the Virginia Constitution (Article 1, Section 3), which underscores the notion of a social compact and the importance of the population's security and protection: "That government is, or ought to be, instituted for the common benefit, protection, and security of the people, nation, or community; of all the various modes and forms of government, that is best which is capable of producing the greatest degree of happiness and safety."[235]

- US and state Supreme Court rulings have often shown that public safety is the first priority of government. In *New York v. Quarles*, the US Supreme Court recognized that the public safety risks produced by a single unsecured gun can outweigh Fifth Amendment rights.[236] In that case, a woman claimed she was raped by an armed man. When the suspect was apprehended, the officer questioned him about the location of his gun without giving Miranda warnings. The Supreme Court refused to exclude the suspect's response as to the location of the gun because the danger created by the gun "presents a situation where concern for public safety must be paramount[.]" The firearm, which the suspect had concealed in a supermarket, posed a potential danger to public safety since an accomplice might use it or an employee might gain possession of it. The Court's ruling regarding the admissibility of the suspect's response showed that the public safety issues raised by a gun in this case outweighed the Fifth Amendment right of suspects.

- A number of state Supreme Court rulings have also taken the position that public safety takes precedence over rights enshrined in the Constitution. In 1874 in the case of *Hill v. State*, the Georgia Supreme Court held that the state's ban on carrying guns in churches, polling places, and courts was constitutional because the right to bear arms does not override safety considerations. That Court would have characterized today's "guns everywhere" laws in states like Georgia as barbaric and as a sign of failure of institutions to protect the public:

It is as well the duty of the general assembly to pass laws for the protection of the person and property of the citizen as it is to abstain from any infringement of the right to bear arms. The preservation of the public peace, and the protection of the people against violence, are constitutional duties of the legislature, and the guarantee of the right to keep and bear arms is to be understood and construed in connection and in harmony with these constitutional duties...To suppose that the framers of the constitution ever dreamed, that in their anxiety to secure to the state a well regulated militia, they were sacrificing the dignity of their courts of justice, the sanctity of their houses of worship, and the peacefulness and good order of their other necessary public assemblies, is absurd. To do so, is to assume that they took it for granted that their whole scheme of law and order, and government and protection, would be a failure, and that the people, instead of depending upon the laws

*and the public authorities for protection, were each man to
take care of himself, and to be always ready to resist to the
death, then and there, all opposers...On the contrary...in
guaranteeing the right to keep and bear arms, they never
dreamed they were authorizing practices, common enough,
it is true, among savages...when every man was at war with
his neighbor, but utterly useless and disgraceful in a well
ordered and civilized community.*[237]

- Similarly, in 1872, the Texas Supreme Court in *English v. State*
  upheld a ban on gun carrying in some circumstances. As in Hill,
  the court took the position that a civilized society should not
  encourage individuals to take the law into their own hands:[238]

*[I]n the great social compact under and by which states and
communities are bound and held together, each individual
has compromised the right to avenge his own wrongs, and
must look to the state for redress. We must not go back to
that state of barbarism in which each claims the right to
administer the law in his own case; that law being simply
the domination of the strong and the violent over the weak
and submissive...It is one of the undisputed functions of
government, to take precautions against crime before it has
been committed, as well as to detect and punish afterwards.*

So much for the idea that only the rights of gun owners should be
considered in public policy. Government has both a social and moral
obligation to protect the public from violence. In addition, as the above
Supreme Court rulings in Georgia and Texas pointed out, policies
encouraging members of the public to carry guns into virtually every
setting bring us back to a state of barbarism and are an admission that our
laws and institutions have failed us in discharging their most fundamental
responsibility—protecting the public from harm.

Guns and the Constitution: The Bottom Line

Throughout most of American history, the courts viewed the Second Amendment as a collective right to form state militias, rather than as the right of individuals to acquire arms. In 2008, the US Supreme Court issued a landmark ruling (*District of Columbia v. Heller*) which broke with this view and held that individuals have a right to possess firearms in the home for a lawful purpose, unconnected with service in a militia. However, the Court held that this right does not extend to anyone for any purpose. The Court made it clear that bans relating to certain categories of people and weapons, as well as uses in "sensitive" settings (e.g., schools), were legitimate forms of regulation. Thus, while the Supreme Court now recognizes gun possession as an individual right, it has made it clear that the type of regulation of guns being proposed by public health and safety advocates (e.g., expanding background checks to all gun buyers, banning assault weapons) does not contravene the Second Amendment.

A substantial body of legal evidence supports the idea that a discussion of rights relating to guns ought not be limited to the rights of gun owners. The Declaration of Independence, the US Constitution, numerous court rulings, and international agreements signed by the US all emphasize the right to life and the duty of government to protect citizens from harm. This is a fundamental aspect of the social contract between citizens and their government. Citizens pay taxes, obey laws, and perform military service when called upon, and the government, in turn, provides protection to citizens. Focusing exclusively on gun rights entirely misses this sacred duty of government.

Chapter 8

THE TRUTH ABOUT GUNS AND FREEDOM

Myth 23: Widespread Gun Ownership and Gun Carrying Increases Our Freedom

The gun lobby considers itself a champion of freedom because it battles for the rights of gun owners. This lobby, along with some gun owners, promotes the view that guns make us freer by helping us ward off attackers. With a gun, they say, we no longer need to rely on police for protection. They also claim that arming civilians allows us to stand up to tyrannical governments.

Fact Check: The view that guns increase our freedom is shattered when one examines the relationship between gun ownership and violence. It is true that in isolated cases a gun may help a person repel an attacker. However, when we move from the individual to the aggregate level, a different view emerges. We find that countries, regions, states, and counties with more guns tend to have higher, not lower, rates of gun death. This is the case because increasing the number of gun owners and carriers in society not only increases defensive gun uses but aggressive and self-destructive uses as well. Unintentional injuries and deaths also increase with higher gun ownership levels. Harmful uses of guns occur many times more frequently than defensive uses (see Chapter 5).

As author Fred Guttenberg notes, he now can only visit his forever-fourteen-year-old daughter at a cemetery. Her rights to life and to freedom have been terminated. The reality of what happened has made his family feel less safe and less free. This is true of many families touched by gun violence around the country. It is a fact that the majority of Americans, including gun owners, believe we must do more to reduce gun violence and to promote responsible use both in the home and in public places. Are we safer and is our freedom enhanced when we have to fear gun violence in schools and expose children to the new reality of active shooter drills? Are we safer and is our freedom enhanced when a shooter can take a weapon and shoot at crowds while hiding out in a hotel? Are we safer and is our freedom enhanced when a shooter can enter a public shopping center with an AR-15? Are we safer and is our freedom enhanced when we are sitting in a place of worship, only to be confronted by an active shooter? Are we safer and is our freedom enhanced when we exercise our First Amendment rights to public demonstration, only to be confronted by armed shooters carrying AR-15s over their shoulders?

Thus, more guns make us less safe and reducing our collective safety makes us less free. Raising the likelihood that we will have our lives extinguished at any moment robs us of our freedom to live our lives fully and to pursue a joyful life. Living with the constant fear of gun violence hanging over our heads is not freedom. The fewer guns there are, the less we have to worry about an encounter that can change our lives in an instant. While arguments and negative encounters occur all the time, there is security in knowing that such encounters are unlikely to lead to disability or death.

The push to arm the maximum number of people in our country raises a concern about our liberties. Gun rights advocates often speak of the importance of their liberty to own the guns they want and to be free of government interference. But wouldn't an armed society take away our freedom to disagree with others on a whole range of issues, from politics to domestic and business matters, or even on such mundane things as who arrived first at a parking spot or the deli counter? If most Americans were armed, would it not be reasonable to fear that, in a dispute, the other person might pull out a gun and use it against us? Even if an armed society did produce a superficial politeness, wouldn't this be at the expense of our basic freedom to express ourselves candidly without the fear of lethal force being used against us?

The gun lobby's efforts to allow guns on college and university campuses have persisted despite polls showing that a majority of campus officials, instructors, students, and police oppose such a policy. Apart from the public safety concern, opponents of guns on campus fear that the presence of guns would have a chilling effect on the ability of professors and students to express themselves freely while discussing the many controversial subjects that are addressed on a college or university campus. Some professors in Texas, for example, have reported avoiding controversial subjects for fear that an armed student who disagrees may become violent.

In my own university criminology courses, we have discussed many hot-button issues such as abortion, racial justice, the death penalty, and many other topics that elicited passionate debate. Some of these topics touched people personally and elicited considerable emotion. I can only imagine how superficial these discussions would have been had students been worried about the possibility that an agitated student would pull out a gun and threaten others.

Campus debates are about reason and persuasion through the force of argument, whereas guns signify power and intimidation through the threat of force. Consider what happened at Utah State University when feminist blogger and media critic Anita Sarkeesian was invited to speak there. Threats were made promising violence, including one that threatened the "deadliest school shooting in American history." The threats, along with the policy of allowing guns on campus, led Sarkeesian to cancel her lecture. Is this the freedom gun rights advocates tell us they support?

Can freedom of speech really prevail in a fully armed society? Would people running for political office or the local school board feel free to express their views on contentious issues if most of the audience was armed? Would members of the audience feel free to ask questions and make comments if everybody around them was armed? Common sense indicates that a fully armed society would be at risk of being a very repressive place in which liberty would be a major casualty. Gun rights advocates also fail to acknowledge that the freedoms enjoyed by gun owners in the US are well in excess of the freedoms accorded in virtually every other advanced society. Most advanced societies have national licensing systems that carefully screen future gun owners, have strict requirements relating to the transportation and storage of guns, and rarely allow people to carry guns for their personal protection.

During the pandemic and following the murder of George Floyd by a Minneapolis police officer, millions of Americans assembled in public places to protest police brutality and systemic racism, as well as to protest public health measures to prevent the spread of COVID-19. A significant number of those protesters were confronted by counter-protesters carrying firearms openly. A study by Everytown for Gun Safety and the Armed Conflict Location & Event Data Project (ACLED) has shown that one in six armed protests that took place from January 2020 through June 2021 turned violent or destructive, and one in sixty-two turned deadly.[239]

Permissive state gun laws explained this phenomenon in part. The study found that the incidence of armed protests was three times higher in states with "expansive open-carry laws."

Such findings point to the perils associated with laws allowing for the open carrying of firearms during protests. While some have argued that open carry will make protests safer, tragedies were far less frequent at protests where guns were not present. The Everytown/ACLED research revealed that, in such cases, just one protest in thirty-seven turned violent or destructive and just one in 2,963 unarmed gatherings proved fatal.

Diana Palmer of Northeastern University conducted a survey on the impact of open carry of firearms on the exercise of protest rights. Palmer found that participants were far less likely to attend a protest, carry a sign, vocalize their views, or bring children to protests if they knew that guns would be present.[240]

When the presence of arms raises the risk of injury, the only people likely to want to participate in public free speech will be either those who are willing to risk their lives, or those inclined to carry weapons in defense of their own right to protest. Rather than serving as a democratizing means of expression, protest may become an armed contest and the exclusive preserve of the non-peaceable. Public protest as we know it may entirely cease to exist. Such a situation would deprive Americans of participating in one of the greatest traditions of this country: expressing their views and advocating for democratic change.

White nationalists who marched in Charlottesville, Virginia, in 2017 discovered that the violence and fatality occurring at the march had consequences with regard to their ability to stage another rally a year later. The city denied them a permit to protest due to fear that the violence would be repeated.[241]

In the last few years, we have seen mass shootings in virtually every type of venue, ranging from residences and workplaces to shopping malls, the streets, airports, nightclubs, schools, colleges, and places of worship. These events are linked to the availability of highly lethal weapons in the US relative to other countries. When one feels highly vulnerable and anxious because personal security is lacking, one cannot be said to be free. Freedom is the condition of being able to lose ourselves in our thoughts, go for a stroll without a worry, and express ourselves without a fear of being harmed, threatened, or shamed by others. A 2019 Harris poll found that a third of Americans avoid certain places or events due to the fear of mass shootings.[242]

Philosopher Firmin Debrabander notes that guns have the effect of chastening speech.[243] He argues that widespread gun carrying would lead us to walk gingerly and watch what we say, how we act, and whom we might offend. He adds that private gun ownership invites retreat into extreme individualism, such as numerous calls for homeschooling in the wake of the Sandy Hook shootings. Such a consequence of these atrocities feeds the illusion that people can police themselves and serve as their own defense force.

However, Debrabander argues that guns undermine the sense of community required to maintain security. Their pervasive, open presence would sow apprehension, suspicion, mistrust and fear, all emotions that are corrosive to community and civic cooperation. He adds that our gun culture promotes a fatal slide into extreme individualism. It fosters a society of individuals who are isolated from one another and paralyzed with fear following every gun-related atrocity. That is not freedom, but its opposite.

America's deadliest mass shooting in a place of worship occurred in Sutherland Springs, Texas, in November 2017. The attack occurred in rural Wilson County, east of San Antonio. In a *New York Times* opinion piece, the pastor of a nearby church wrote:

> The idea that such a thing would happen in a sacred space, a place where families are supposed to be safe, has angered many people. Churches are places where the spirit of God is felt, where the presence of God is very real, where manners are expected and vulgarity is shunned. The church is where we, with all our faults and failures, come into the presence of the divine to find grace, to find peace, to rest in the arms of the Lord. The church is a sanctuary in the literal sense of the word, set apart, safe, protecting. All this was shattered.

> Those who moved to the country to protect their family from the perceived dangers of the city were especially shaken. Almost every family here identifies with a church. In some cases, it's more a matter of a family tradition than active participation. But for weddings and funerals, it is usually the "family church" that's called. Even so, families go to different churches as they find activities that fit their needs. The Boy Scouts at the Methodist church. Soccer at the Roman Catholic church. Lions Club meetings at the Church of Christ. One church has a clinic while another has a day care and still another a weekly lunch for the elderly. The churches work together to run a food bank, sponsor blood drives, and hold community worship services on Thanksgiving and Good Friday.[244]

The availability of weapons designed for the military enable the type of massacre seen in Sutherland Springs. Communities are shattered. The inability to worship in a safe environment due to the threat of mass shootings is anything but freedom.

Some of the gun lobby's initiatives in recent years have suppressed rather than promoted freedom. Polls show that their efforts to allow guns on campus in a number of states are at odds with the wishes of the vast majority of campus administrators, faculty, and students.[245] Preemption laws prevent local governments from passing their own gun laws. How do these laws contribute to the freedom of counties wishing to pass laws to protect their constituents from violence? Concealed carry reciprocity would allow individuals from states with very weak laws—including those without permits—to seamlessly cross state lines with guns and to carry them in states with much stricter gun laws. Again, this would be the central authority of the federal government imposing more lax gun laws on states which have stronger gun laws. Then there are the physician gag laws that have prohibited doctors from discussing gun safety with their patients, seemingly a violation of the First Amendment right to free speech.

About three-quarters of Americans do not own firearms, and their desire to live in gun-free settings must also be respected. America's continuing paralysis in relation to gun policy and our failure to respond effectively to gun violence means that the trend of more frequent and extreme acts of violence will continue until meaningful reform occurs. As long as we remain on the current path, some people will limit their own activities out of fear, security measures that restrict our freedoms will be stepped up, and our privacy will be increasingly compromised by more surveillance of our movements and communications. This is an erosion of our freedoms, rather than the reverse.

Consider the cancellation in August 2022 of an annual music festival in midtown Atlanta, reportedly due to the extremely permissive gun laws in Georgia. The cancellation of the festival meant that the community's freedom to enjoy this annual event was curtailed, and the cost to the local economy was estimated to be approximately 50 million dollars. Organizers cancelled the festival because Georgia gun laws would not allow them to prevent people from carrying guns into the event, thereby safeguarding attendees.[246]

The gun lobby and a number of local law enforcement officials have begun a "Second Amendment sanctuary" movement.[247] As of January, 2020, more than 400 municipalities in twenty states have passed resolutions declaring that they would not enforce certain "unconstitutional" gun laws passed by the federal government or the state. These local governments are basically saying that they can pick and choose the federal and state laws they wish to uphold, a view that is regarded by constitutional experts as having no merit.

Mary B. McCord, a former acting assistant attorney general for national security, has argued that Second Amendment sanctuary resolutions have no legal basis and that only a court can overturn a state or federal law. She notes that state constitutions, statutes, and common law generally affirm the "supremacy" of federal and state law.[248] This movement is therefore one that defies the Constitution and the rule of law. How can defiance of the rule of law in a democratic country and the undermining of democracy be viewed as promoting freedom?

Myth 24: We Must Choose between Public Safety and the Freedom to Own Guns

One key myth is that we have to choose between respecting the rights of gun owners to possess firearms and gun regulations that can save lives and enhance public safety.

Fact Check: This is a false choice and leads to the argument that there is no compromise, and that one side must prevail and the other lose in relation to gun policy. Such a narrative opens the door to extremists who argue that any gun law is a violation of gun rights.

This is patent nonsense. One can keep a gun in the home and store it safely, thereby preventing children and teenagers from gaining access to it. Gun suicides by young people are on the rise[249] and school shootings are problematic. Many of the guns used in these tragedies were obtained from the shooter's home. One can also own a gun that is equipped with features that can prevent deadly accidents, such as magazine safeties and loaded chamber indicators. We can carefully screen prospective gun owners for instability and a history of violence while continuing to grant stable, nonviolent people access to guns. We can ban or more tightly regulate weapons designed for the military and law enforcement— semiautomatic rifles and pistols fed by high-capacity magazines—while allowing wide access to firearms that cannot shoot thirty-five people in thirty seconds as was the case in Dayton, Ohio, in the summer of 2019. We already have federal and state regulations that have been upheld by the courts as constitutional while leaving far more access to guns by most citizens than is the case in other countries.

Messaging by those seeking reform in this area must show that this polarized thinking; the idea that either you have gun rights or gun regulation is false and merely fuels the paralysis in our ability to deal with gun violence. This plays right into the hands of those who wish to do nothing about the violence.

Myth 25: Gun Violence Is the Price We Pay for Our Freedoms.

Following the Century Theater mass shooting in Aurora, Colorado, Professor James Alan Fox, one of America's leading criminologists, stated: "Mass murder is regrettably one of the painful consequences of the freedoms we enjoy."[250] Fox is suggesting here that mass murder goes with personal freedoms and cannot be avoided.

Fact Check: While some mass murder will always exist, other free countries have adopted measures, such as licensing gun owners and banning especially dangerous weapons, that have reduced the number of gun deaths. The US has about 11,000 gun homicides each year. By contrast, the United Kingdom has about 40 gun homicides a year, Australia has 35, Germany approximately 60, and Japan about ten.[251] These are all democratic countries. When we combine other advanced countries and adjust for population differences, the US has a gun homicide rate twenty-five times higher than other advanced democracies.[252] America further stands alone in terms of the rates at which women, children, and youth are killed with the use of guns.

We are also an outlier when it comes to mass shootings. In 2021, the Gun Violence Archive reported nearly 700 mass shootings in the US—almost an astounding two per day![253] A third of all the civilian mass shootings in the world occur in the US even though we have just 5 percent of the world's population.

When Professor Fox says that mass murder is the price we pay for our freedoms, he seems to be suggesting that our right to own guns with few restrictions is worth sacrificing our right to life and to enjoy a normal life free of constant threats with guns. The freedom to own guns and personal safety can be pursued simultaneously; we do not have to choose one or the other, but we do need to compromise. We can do more to ensure that people at a high risk of committing violent crimes do not get access to lethal weapons. We can require that gun owners store guns safely, and we can equip guns with safety features that will prevent deadly accidents.

The notion of freedom should include our ability to go to work and school, worship, and move around in our communities safely without getting shot. The right to life, also expressed in the Declaration of Independence, is one of our most fundamental freedoms, and unregulated gun ownership and gun carrying place it at risk. Is it truly freedom when we are constantly at risk of being shot and killed? Is it really freedom when parents fear that their kids going out to a club or off to school might not return due to gun violence? It is a warped view of freedom to value above all the right to unregulated gun ownership without considering the freedom to enjoy a life without the ever present worry that we or our loved ones may have our lives extinguished at any moment.

Statements justifying gun violence in America as the price of freedom are especially absurd when we examine international rankings of the freedoms enjoyed in different countries. One ranking, examining civil and political rights in 210 countries, found the US to rank below fiftieth in the world.[254] Surely America's permissive gun laws and high levels of gun mortality are not justified by such a poor showing on freedoms for ordinary people.

Guns and Freedom: The Bottom Line

- The idea that permissive gun laws and more guns promote freedom and civility in society is misguided. Yes, permissive laws increase the freedom of a minority to own guns, but this comes at a high price with regard to both the freedom and security of the general public. Studies consistently show that more guns are usually accompanied by more gun deaths, whether we are comparing nations, regions, or states. Guns therefore pose a threat to the freedom to live our lives without being shot.

- It is contradictory to speak of civility being achieved through a threat or the use of force with a firearm. Guns are designed to intimidate and harm, rather than to achieve civility or mutual respect. The carrying of guns stifles free speech and expression, whether the setting is a university, a protest, a public meeting, or anywhere a dispute is taking place. Widespread gun ownership and gun carrying for self-protection fosters extreme individualism that is corrosive to community life. Higher levels of fear associated with wider gun ownership and the inevitably resulting violence lead to a greater demand for police, private security, and surveillance to maintain order. This is not more freedom but an erosion of liberty.

- Surveys show the impact of open carry of firearms on the exercise of protest rights. One study found that participants were far less likely to attend a protest, carry a sign, vocalize their views, or bring children to protests if they knew that guns would be present. Many Americans have also stated they avoid certain places or events due to the fear of mass shootings.

- It is a false choice to argue that one must either support gun rights or gun regulation. Such a narrative opens the door to extremists who argue that any gun law is a violation of gun rights. Guns can be stored safely and still be available for self-defense. They can also be equipped with safety features. We can carefully screen prospective gun owners for instability and a history of violence while continuing to grant stable, nonviolent people access to guns. Weapons designed for the military and law enforcement can be banned or more tightly regulated while wide access is still available to firearms not capable of large-scale massacres in a matter of a few minutes.

- The notion that high levels of gun violence are the price we pay for freedom has little credibility. While some mass murder will always exist, other free countries have adopted measures, such as licensing gun owners and banning especially dangerous weapons, that have reduced the number of gun deaths. In fact, many countries with a higher freedom ranking than America have much lower levels of gun violence as a result of the type of regulations just mentioned.

Chapter 9

THE TRUTH AS TO WHY GUNS OUGHT TO BE REGULATED

Myth 26: We Need to Tackle the Root Causes of Violence and Stop Blaming Guns

Fact Check: The above statement takes the position that understanding violence is an "either/or" proposition. That is, it asserts that we have to choose between what people call "root causes," which we assume means factors like poverty and mental illness, and the widespread availability of guns. This simplistic and naïve view of violence does not allow for the possibility that a person's violent behavior may be due to a combination of factors. In the medical field, for example, the Mayo Clinic tells us that risk factors for coronary artery disease include age, gender, family history, smoking, physical inactivity, obesity, high stress, high blood pressure, high cholesterol levels, diabetes, and an unhealthy diet.[255] When many of these risk factors are present, the chances of developing heart disease and suffering a heart attack are greater than if just one factor is present. So it is not inactivity versus an unhealthy diet. The more of these risk factors one has, the greater the likelihood that one will develop heart disease.

In the same way, many criminologists agree that there are both background factors that place one at risk of violence as well as more immediate factors present in any given time or place that may lead to the decision to commit a crime and influence its severity. Poverty, temperament, family, and community factors have long been known to play a role in someone's likelihood of engaging in crime. These are some of the so-called root causes. In addition, over the last thirty years, there has been an increasing recognition that situational factors (ones that are more immediate and proximal) may influence the decision to commit a crime at any particular time.[256]

Situational factors that may influence the decision to commit violence or other crimes include:

- Whether the individual is under the influence of drugs or alcohol

- Presence of others who may intervene to stop a crime or conflict or who may facilitate it

- Presence of an opportunity to commit a violent or criminal act

- Risks of being harmed or apprehended by police

- The availability of a gun

The presence of lethal weapons has long been viewed as a factor determining whether a crime can be committed against a certain target (e.g., a protected or armed target) and the likelihood of a fatality if the crime occurs. Guns can make it easier to assault multiple people at once (as in mass or gang-related shootings), to inflict injury at a distance (drive-by shooting), or to assault someone when one is too squeamish to harm another person from close range.[257] A survey of 100 incarcerated violent offenders found that conflicts were far more likely to escalate to violence when the individual had a gun on hand.[258] Most importantly, multiple studies have shown that the use of a firearm in a dispute also increases the likelihood of death relative to other weapons (e.g., knives and blunt objects).[259]

The evidence shows that apart from root causes and individual intent, the presence of a firearm also has an independent effect on the decision to commit violence and on its lethality. It is therefore not sufficient to focus only on the root causes of violence since the presence and use of guns in a conflict or other incident is an enormous factor in the occurrence, severity, and the number of victims of violence.

Myth 27: Why Ban Guns When People Can Also be Killed with Knives or a Frozen Ham, or Die in a Car or Pool?

Fact Check: First of all, no credible group is proposing the banning of all guns or the complete disarmament of Americans. This is a bogus argument, and any total ban on guns would contravene the Second Amendment according to the most recent Supreme Court rulings. Yes, some groups are proposing banning certain models of firearms, such as semiautomatic rifles designed for the military.

Second, consumer items like cars that are involved in about an equal number of deaths as guns are heavily regulated, and many measures are in place nationally to reduce accidents, with great success. People are normally required to obtain a license and insurance after passing a driving test, cars must meet safety standards, road safety measures and speeding laws have been implemented, driving while drinking is illegal, research is supported by the federal government, and a federal agency, the National Highway Traffic Safety Administration, regulates the safety of motor vehicles. Due to all these efforts, there has been a 95 percent decline over the last century in car-related deaths per 100 million miles driven.[260] By contrast, guns, unlike other consumer items, are exempt from oversight by the Consumer Products Safety Commission, there is no federal program aiming to make them safer or of higher quality, and federal gun research has been obstructed since 1996 by members of Congress working on behalf of the gun lobby.[261]

We often hear opponents of gun laws asking why we don't ban knives, swimming pools, and other products, since knives can kill and people drown in pools each year. Even a frozen ham, they say, can be used to kill. Again, nobody is proposing to ban guns. Also, unlike guns, knives and pools are regulated, or at least in the case of pools, the CPSC participates in the development of safety standards. Have you ever heard of a mass killing with a ham?

There is a fundamental difference between guns and consumer products like cars, knives, and pools. Cars are designed for transportation, knives are usually used for cutting food, and pools are designed for recreation. Most deaths and injuries associated with these products are unintentional. By contrast, guns are designed to kill humans or game. Handguns are normally designed for self-defense. Assault-style rifles like the AR-15 have a muzzle velocity, range, light weight, and rate of fire that enable killing multiple individuals at a distance. While unintentional injuries and deaths do occur with guns, most gun deaths are intentional, whether they are inflicted against others or self-inflicted.

Ironically, despite being the only consumer product designed for killing, the gun industry is the only one that has been shielded from liability when people are injured or killed by their products.[262] No other industry benefits from such protection.

There has been no serious attempt to ban guns; therefore, the premise of the statement is misleading. Unlike cars, knives, and other consumer items, guns are designed to kill and do so efficiently. Cars and other consumer items, such as toys, appliances, and mattresses, are subject to consumer regulation to ensure public safety, while guns are not. There is no logical reason for guns to escape such oversight as guns are lethal products and safety standards could prevent deaths and injuries. The process that exempted guns from such oversight was a political one.

Myth 28: Guns Don't Matter Because People Will Find a Way to Kill Others or Themselves Regardless of Gun Availability

This is the method substitution argument; the idea that people determined to harm others or themselves will do so regardless of gun laws or the availability of guns. Therefore, according to this line of argument, laws limiting the availability of guns are futile.

Fact Check: The key term above is "determined." Yes, the method substitution argument may have considerable merit if we consider only those cases in which somebody has a longstanding and unwavering desire to harm another or themselves. Over time, they will likely identify another method to achieve their aim if they have a powerful and enduring desire to do harm. There are certainly other means of committing a homicide or suicide than with a gun.

However, most homicides and suicides do not fit this description. Most homicides are not "first degree" murders, involving premeditation (planning) and deliberation (careful consideration of options and consequences). Rather, they are often "second degree" murders, in which premeditation is lacking and harm, but not a murder, was intended, or where the assailant showed a profound indifference to life (e.g., firing into a crowd in a fit of anger). Or they are cases of "manslaughter," where an individual becomes violent in the "heat of passion" or responds to a sudden provocation with violence. Involuntary manslaughter or criminally negligent homicide is one in which an individual behaves recklessly or in a negligent fashion and causes the death of another (celebratory gunfire that accidentally kills someone).

Thus, most forms of homicide do not involve premeditation and are often impulsive. It is in the case of disputes that erupt spontaneously that the nature of the weapons possessed by the parties is most critical. As guns are three to five times as likely to be lethal than knives and many more times as lethal as other weapons, the presence of a gun in fights or arguments that arise suddenly raises the likelihood that someone will die.[263]

With suicide, contrary to popular belief, the vast majority of those attempting to take their own lives do not display an unwavering determination to do so. Suicidologists have found that just 10–15 percent of people who commit suicide demonstrate such a determination to die. Psychologist Kay R. Jamison, a specialist in mood disorders at Johns Hopkins University, notes that most suicidal individuals are ambivalent about dying. She believes that, at most, 10–15 percent of suicide cases are characterized by an unwavering determination to die on the part of the victim. For others, the risk is transient.[264]

Numerous studies show that suicides are often impulsive, as the decision to attempt suicide often occurs just a few minutes or hours prior to the attempt. Also, there is frequently great ambivalence about suicide, rather than a single-minded determination to die. Many individuals who make serious attempts but survive do not repeat their attempts. This frequent impulsivity, ambivalence, and regret mean that the presence of lethal methods when an attempt is made may be a crucial factor in whether an individual succeeds in taking his or her life. There are enormous differences in the lethality of methods, with firearms consistently found to be the most lethal of them all—about 90 percent lethal, as opposed to 2–3 percent in the case of an overdose.

There is abundant evidence that suicide methods are often chosen on the basis of their availability. Many cases show that we cannot assume that people will switch to similarly lethal methods when their chosen method becomes unavailable.

In certain regions of Asia and the Pacific Islands, pesticides are among the most common suicide methods. In Sri Lanka, controlling the availability of highly lethal pesticides such as paraquat has brought about dramatic reductions in the overall suicide rate, indicating that large-scale substitution of other lethal methods did not occur or that attempts with less lethal products resulted in fewer deaths. The fatality rate of attempts using paraquat has been reported to be over 60 percent, whereas it may be below 10 percent for other pesticides that have replaced paraquat.[265]

One of the best examples of what can be achieved when an easily available and highly lethal means of suicide is eliminated occurred when the domestic gas supply was changed in the UK. Before 1958, domestic gas was toxic, containing over 12 percent carbon monoxide. People would commit suicide simply by putting their heads in their ovens. In 1958, nontoxic natural gas was introduced region by region, and, by 1974, virtually all the gas supply in the UK was nontoxic. Prior to the changeover, suicide by gas inhalation was the leading means of suicide in the UK. Keith Hawton of Oxford University notes that as the carbon monoxide content of gas supplies decreased, there was a steady reduction in carbon monoxide suicides in England and Wales. While there was a modest increase in the use of other suicide methods, the overall suicide rate decreased by a third. A similar pattern was observed in Scotland.

Hawton believes that thousands of lives were saved simply by detoxifying the domestic gas supply.[266]

Therefore, much of what we know about suicide indicates that reducing access to highly lethal methods, such as firearms, is likely to lead to a reduction in suicides. This is the case because some people do not switch to other highly lethal methods. If they switch to a method that is not likely to result in death, a suicide may be averted, since many do not repeat their suicide attempts.

Why Guns Should Be Regulated: The Bottom Line

- Understanding crime is not an either/or proposition; it would be illogical to focus either solely on root causes or on the immediate circumstances just prior to an offense. Both are important. Poverty, temperament, family, and community factors have long been known to play a role in someone's likelihood of engaging in crime. These are some of the so-called root causes. In addition, over the last thirty years, there has been an increasing emphasis on understanding situational (more immediate and proximal) factors that may influence the decision to commit a crime at a particular time. Among these factors is the presence or absence of guns. Guns can enable violence as well as mass violence, and, when they are used to attack others, they increase the likelihood of a fatality. It is therefore not sufficient to focus on root causes of violence because the presence and use of guns in a conflict or other incident is a critical factor in the occurrence, severity, and number of victims of violence.

- Like other consumer products, guns need to be regulated. While people can be killed with many weapons and also can die in car crashes and pools, guns are lethal products specifically designed to kill. Most deaths and injuries associated with products like cars and pools are unintentional. By contrast, guns are designed to kill humans or game. Handguns are normally designed for self-defense. Assault-style rifles like the AR-15 have a muzzle velocity, range, light weight, and rate of fire that enable killing multiple individuals at a distance. While unintentional injuries and deaths do occur with guns, most gun deaths are intentional, whether they are inflicted against others or self-inflicted. Guns therefore deserve special regulatory attention, but they have instead been exempted from oversight by the Consumer Product Safety Commission, and, unlike other industries, federal law shields gun manufacturers from lawsuits when the products they make are used to kill.

- The weapons substitution argument, the notion that gun regulation is futile because individuals will merely commit homicide or suicide with other weapons, is not supported by the evidence. This argument is based on the false assumption that most people who kill others or commit suicide have contemplated doing so for a long time and are sufficiently determined that they can find the means to accomplish their goals if firearms are not available. In reality, most homicides arise from disputes that often erupt suddenly, and many suicides are attempted with little consideration and during a personal crisis. The availability of firearms during these times can make all the difference in the outcome of assaults and suicide attempts.

Chapter 10

THE TRUTH ABOUT GUN LAWS AND GUN VIOLENCE PREVENTION

Myth 29: Gun Violence Prevention Always Involves Changes to Laws and Public Money

Fact Check: There are many gun violence initiatives that do not involve law reforms, and many others require little or no public funding. Consider first law enforcement strategies that do involve public funding but are focused on improving the enforcement of crime without changes to laws.

One example is an enforcement strategy called "hot spot" policing. Criminologists have learned that routine police patrols are not very effective since they cover an entire area equally—although crime is not distributed equally—and are spread too thinly to make much of a difference. This approach of just cruising through an area rarely intercepts crimes in progress and serves as only a minimal deterrent due to the small number of passes by any location. In general, it just reassures citizens that law enforcement officers are there for them.

A new approach complements routine patrols with an intensive focus on highly active neighborhoods, blocks, or even smaller sites (e.g., bus terminals). These crime "hot spots" are identified through crime mapping. Police officers are deployed to these areas in greater numbers and engage in crime suppression activities, as well as efforts to deal with the underlying causes of crime at that location. For example, in 2009, the Philadelphia Police Department participated in an experiment in which foot patrols were deployed in pairs to the most troublesome intersections in the city. Officers spoke to residents, visited juvenile hangouts, and stopped known lawbreakers in their cars and on sidewalks. In the program's first three months, there was a 23 percent reduction in reported violent crime in these hot spots compared with similar areas not receiving the extra foot patrols.[267] In the areas targeted by the experiment, enforcement actions (arrests, pedestrian and vehicle stops, disruptions of disturbances, and narcotics enforcement) increased, likely deterring violence. However, once the experiment was over and the foot patrols were removed from the crime hot spots, the impact of the foot patrols was not sustained.

Another enforcement strategy not requiring changes in the law is the formation of gun squads designed to get illegal weapons off the streets of especially violent neighborhoods. These specialized squads use intelligence to identify individuals who may possess illegal weapons. They encourage community members to provide tips on individuals who may be carrying illegally, and they frequently stop individuals and cars to search them for weapons. Over a twenty-nine-week period in Kansas City, gun seizures increased by 65 percent, and gun crimes, including homicides, fell by 49 percent without any evidence that crime spilled over into adjacent neighborhoods.[268]

Another approach to preventing gun violence is a community-based, nongovernmental approach referred to as "violence interruption." Again, this approach requires no changes in the law. Much violence, including a significant share of mass shootings, involves conflicts and cycles of retaliation among individuals and small groups. One immediate way of preventing violence is interrupting these cycles by working with people who have been victimized or those who may seek revenge on behalf of the injured or deceased individual. Hospital-based violence intervention programs seek to reduce violence by focusing on high-risk individuals recently admitted to a hospital for a violent injury. Medical professionals know that being the victim of a violent injury makes it far more likely that the person will return with a subsequent injury or become a perpetrator of violence.

Hospitalization for a serious injury may represent a unique opportunity to intervene positively. Currently, hospitals discharge patients injured from gunshot wounds without any strategy to address the increased likelihood of violence. Where there is an intervention program, patients are screened to identify those at greatest risk and matched with case managers who provide intense oversight both at the hospital and in the critical months following their release from the hospital. At the same time, the case managers help connect their clients with community agencies providing a range of services, including introducing high-risk individuals to a variety of community-based organizations to help them gain access to employment, housing, and educational resources. An evaluation of the YouthAlive! Program in Oakland, California, found its clients were 70 percent less likely to be arrested and 60 percent less likely to have any criminal involvement compared to a control group.[269] A Baltimore program found that just 5 percent of participating patients were reinjured, compared to 36 percent for non-participants. Participants were also four times less likely to be convicted of a crime than non-participants.[270]

There are also many citizen-based anti-violence initiatives that require little or no public funding. With a group of committed volunteers, the support of local agencies, and perhaps some limited fundraising, programs can be launched without delay that impose little or no financial burden on public agencies.

Some examples:

- **Securing Guns in the Home.** In Broward County, Florida, attorney Barbara Markley and fellow members of the Gun Safety Committee of the League of Women Voters (LWV) initiated Lock It Up, a program that is rapidly gaining more partners. League members learned that the Veterans Administration maintains a large inventory of trigger locks due to the elevated suicide risk for veterans. The VA has donated thousands of locks to the LWV, which is distributing them to a wide variety of agencies and professionals, including law enforcement, municipalities, libraries, churches, pediatricians, family therapy and university clinics, and daycare centers. They also have produced a brochure to raise awareness about the dangers of unlocked guns around children and teens.

- **Gun Buybacks.** Gun buybacks allow people to turn in guns, usually to the police, for an incentive of cash or gift cards with no questions asked. They provide the public an opportunity to relinquish weapons that are not being used, are possessed illegally, or that may be a danger to households. In some cases, hundreds of guns have been turned in. Most initiatives involve law enforcement agencies, which receive the guns, and some partner with physicians and medical centers that can counsel gun owners about safety. At a recent event in Hillsborough County, Florida, the Sheriff's Office received 1,173 guns in five hours, including some stolen guns.[271] At a previous event in that county, 2,541 guns were turned in.

- **Consumer Activism.** Consumers can pressure stores to refrain from selling military-style and other highly lethal weapons through letter-writing campaigns, personal appeals to store managers and executives, social media campaigns on Facebook and Twitter, and boycotts. Individuals and pension funds can also refuse to buy and divest from gun stocks or mutual funds containing gun stocks until those companies stop selling military-style weapons and start producing weapons with certain safety features (e.g., magazine safeties, loaded chamber indicators) and personalized (smart) weapons.

- **Investor Activism.** Given the targeting of several campuses by mass shooters, some academics are demanding that their retirement funds be "gun-free."[272] In one initiative, more than 4,000 faculty members threatened a firm managing their funds with the transfer of their money to gun-free funds if the firm continued to invest in companies that manufacture assault-style weapons. In another example, driven by outrage over the school shooting in Parkland, Florida, and backed by some of America's largest institutional investors, Sister Judy Byron of Seattle and a small group of shareholders forced two gun manufacturers, Sturm Ruger and American Outdoor Brands, to produce reports detailing the use of their guns in violent crimes and showing what steps the companies are taking to develop safer weapons.[273] Although the companies urged their shareholders to reject the proposals, a majority sided with the activists.

- **Supporting Victims of Abuse.** The REACH program in Massachusetts has an Emergency Shelter Program providing crisis intervention and support services for victims of domestic violence who are not safe in their own home.[274] Services include assistance with finding longer-term housing, support with legal issues, and access to other resources to help families heal physically and emotionally. REACH's Community-Based Advocacy Program offers a similar range of services to domestic violence survivors who do not want to leave an abusive relationship or who are not seeking shelter. The charitable organization also can help with safety planning, finding a job or housing, or accessing benefits.

- **Public Education Initiatives.** Educating the public about gun safety can include tips for making their homes safer (such as securing guns with trigger locks or other locking devices) and awareness of the steps they need to take to protect their children when visiting the homes of gun owners. Safety presentations, videos, written materials on gun violence and safety, and public service announcements can shift public opinion, especially when done on a large scale.

Over the last three decades, the gun lobby has been successful in selling the idea that guns make us safer from violence. Pew Research Center reports that in 1993 just 34 percent of Americans said it was more important to protect gun rights than to control gun ownership, but by 2014, some of its polling showed that number had climbed to 52 percent.[275] Increasing grassroots activity, including educational efforts on the part of groups favoring tighter regulation of guns, may reverse this trend. Thoughtful and evidence-based letters to the editor and other media commentary also can have a cumulative effect on public opinion.

- **Donations.** Individuals seeking to make a difference can make a donation to an anti-violence organization or program, a trauma center, programs aiding victims of violence, or institutes conducting research on violence. One can also donate to political candidates with serious anti-gun violence platforms.

- **Voting.** One of the easiest steps people can take to effect change is to vote. Informed voters can support candidates who are committed to serious legal reforms. This means that they don't merely offer vague, general statements about their commitment to the prevention of gun violence. Rather, they commit to specific policies, such as the licensing of gun owners and the banning of weapons designed for war. That way, they can be held accountable if they fail to support these policies when they get into office.

One useful tool to determine where candidates stand on guns is gunsensevoter.org. On that site, the large grassroots group Moms Demand Action for Gun Sense in America endorses candidates who support laws shown to be effective in combatting gun violence.

Myth 30: Switzerland and Israel Have Relaxed Gun Laws and Low Murder Rates

Gun rights advocates argue that it is not guns but societal factors that lead to high levels of violence. To bolster this argument, they cite two countries which have what they believe are relaxed gun laws yet have escaped high rates of gun violence. For example, Wayne LaPierre of the NRA has written that Switzerland has a higher rate of firearms possession than the US and very few gun homicides. LaPierre states that this demonstrates that "...there is no causal effect between firearms possession and crime. Indeed, just the opposite seems to be the case: A thoroughly armed people is relatively crime free; it is the ultimate deterrent to crime."[276]

Fact Check: Even if LaPierre's observations were correct, identifying one or two countries that break with a pattern does not disprove the pattern. It is like saying that if we can identify a few people who have lived to an advanced age despite drinking and smoking excessively, we can demonstrate that these habits have no adverse health effects. Just as alcohol and nicotine consumption are not the only factors determining one's longevity, gun availability is not the only factor shaping a country's rates of violence. In some cases, very positive or negative social forces may override the impact of gun availability, but that doesn't mean that the extent to which guns are available has no impact.

However, LaPierre and other opponents of tighter gun regulations misrepresent the role of guns in both Switzerland and Israel. First, the Geneva-based Small Arms Survey shows that the US has many more civilian-held guns per capita (120 guns per 100 people) than either Switzerland (27 guns per 100 people) or Israel (6.7 per 100 people).[277] In both countries, firearms are usually kept for military purposes or in relation to security functions rather than for hunting, collecting, or self-protection as in America. Switzerland and Israel both have systems of military conscription. In Switzerland, all males are required to undertake military service from the age of nineteen, beginning with a five-month stint and continuing with annual refresher courses for at least another ten years. In Israel, most men and women must perform military service from the age of eighteen. Men serve for three years and then participate in the reserves until the age of fifty-one, and women serve for twenty-one months.

Contrary to the impression given by the NRA's LaPierre, regulations are very strict in both Switzerland and Israel. In Switzerland, guns must be stored unloaded and kept in a locked cabinet, and citizens are subject to regular inspections of their guns. The purchase of a handgun requires a license in Switzerland, and just 4 percent of national survey respondents have indicated they keep their guns for self-protection.[278] Currently, less than a quarter of former soldiers elect to keep their weapons once their military service has been completed.

In Israel, civilian gun ownership levels are a fraction of those in the US, despite the fact that most adults have served in the military. Almost half of gun permit applicants are rejected, and licenses are only issued to security personnel, those transporting valuables and explosives, hunters, and West Bank residents. Handgun purchases require psychological checks and an extended waiting period.[279] Neither country provides a good example of permissive gun laws, as they are in fact examples of the opposite. The US has both significantly higher civilian gun ownership levels and substantially higher rates of gun homicide than either country. Guns in both countries are primarily maintained to protect the country from its enemies, rather than individuals from their fellow citizens as in America.

Myth 31: Hitler Introduced Strict Gun Control to Repress the Population

This claim makes the point that disarmament ultimately enables the formation of authoritarian regimes because guns are a citizenry's best protection from tyranny. There is a fairly widespread belief that Adolph Hitler confiscated all guns and was able to repress the population by doing so. Ben Carson, former US Secretary of Housing and Urban Development, made the following erroneous statement, later repeated by many others: "German citizens were disarmed by their government in the late 1930s, [which allowed the Nazis to] carry out their evil intentions with relatively little resistance."[280]

Fact Check: Strict gun control in Germany had its origins in the years following World War I. In an attempt to stabilize the country and to comply with the Treaty of Versailles, the German government in 1919 enacted legislation requiring the surrender of all firearms to the government. In 1928, before the rise of Hitler's Nazi regime, the government repealed the ban on firearms possession and implemented a licensing system requiring separate permits to own or sell firearms, carry firearms, manufacture firearms, or professionally deal in firearms and ammunition. Within the span of a decade, Germany had shifted from a severe firearms seizure policy to a modern, comprehensive system of regulations.[281]

In 1938, the Nazi regime passed the *Weapons Law,* which has been incorrectly depicted by the NRA in the US and pro-gun advocates as a draconian law that disarmed the German population. In fact, while the law did prohibit the Jewish population in Germany from possessing, manufacturing, and dealing in firearms, the Nazi regime did not disarm over 99 percent of the population, which was non-Jewish.[282] The regime maintained a system of licensing and even relaxed certain regulations. For example, the regime lowered the age at which people could own guns, increased the validity period of carry permits, and increased the number of groups exempted from obtaining an acquisition permit.[283] **Thus, in theory at least,** the vast majority of citizens of Germany could have offered an armed resistance to their fascist government, but did not do so. Hitler did not support gun prohibition.

Myth 32: We Don't Need More Gun Laws, We Just Need to Enforce the Laws We Have

One creative objection to additional gun regulation is the idea that there are already numerous gun laws that are poorly enforced. Therefore, it is argued that rather than more gun laws, we need better enforcement.

Fact Check: This is a clever argument because it leaves the impression that proponents support gun regulation and lament the poor enforcement of existing laws. When using this argument, gun rights advocates do not attack gun regulation and in fact pretend to support gun safety measures and laws. This line of argument also falsely suggests that gun regulation continues to grow, whereas many laws have actually weakened regulation and made it easier to carry guns, obtain permits, and use lethal force. There is also a growing movement in the states—twenty-five at last count—to eliminate all permitting requirements for those carrying guns.

Among other things, this development means that individuals carrying lethal weapons will not be required to have any education or training whatsoever on what constitutes legitimate self-defense, nor in the use and safe handling of firearms.

Let's be clear here. Not all laws place restrictions on the possession or purchase of firearms. Gun laws also limit inspections of gun dealers, prevent localities/counties from passing their own laws (preemption), ensure that guns are not subject to consumer protection laws and oversight, and shield the gun industry from liability when guns are used in shootings and mass killings. It should also be stressed that many gun laws and bills being proposed are popular with the public but are blocked by a powerful lobby and/or members of Congress representing a minority of citizens.

The gun lobby has, in fact, undermined the enforcement of laws at many levels, thereby helping people obtain guns illegally. The NRA has opposed closing the loophole that allows those buying guns on the private market—at gun shows or online—to avoid a criminal background check. As a result, many guns involved in federal gun trafficking investigations have a gun show connection, and many investigations find gun shows where felons are buying and selling guns.[284] Many prison inmates tell us that they obtained their weapons on the private, unregulated market.

Also, legislation backed by the gun lobby limits the number of inspections of gun dealers the ATF can make each year, thereby impeding efforts to control gun trafficking and the sale of guns to prohibited persons. Oversight of dealers is important, since many gun dealers have admitted to selling to individuals who stated that they could not pass a background check or have been found to have sold weapons to "straw purchasers," people buying firearms on behalf of others who can't pass background checks.[285] Furthermore, the Bureau of Alcohol, Tobacco, Firearms, and Explosives did not have a permanent director for seven years, due to an

NRA-backed requirement that the Senate approve nominees. ATF also is severely starved of resources, and the DOJ Office of the Inspector General concluded that it would take twenty-two years to inspect all federally licensed dealers.[286] Political pressure exerted by friends of the gun lobby has much to do with this situation.

One of the NRA's greatest victories was its campaign to weaken the Gun Control Act of 1968 through a series of amendments called the Firearm Owners Protection Act (FOPA), an act that protects gun dealers rather than owners. FOPA set a very high standard of proof to demonstrate that a dealer had committed a criminal violation and to revoke a dealer's license. The government must now show a willful violation of the law, which means that it must prove both that it was intentional and that the violator knew the conduct was unlawful. FOPA also helped dealers engaged in lawbreaking by reclassifying violations of federal record keeping laws from felonies to misdemeanors. How records are kept is critical because tracing guns can only be done if dealers comply with requirements in this area.

A provision of the 1986 Firearm Owners Protection Act bans states or federal agencies from building gun registries. Congress has also protected gun manufacturers from lawsuits at the behest of the gun lobby following lawsuits by cities against the gun industry. Threats from the NRA blocked the Centers for Disease Control from researching gun deaths for twenty-five years.

Rather than helping enforcement, the NRA has undermined the ability of Brady background checks to keep lawbreakers from being armed. In the early 2000s, a rule was adopted by the Bush administration requiring that records pertaining to background checks conducted in firearms sales that were allowed to proceed be destroyed within 24 hours. Attorney Dennis Henigan writes:

There is no question that the twenty-four-hour rule has helped to arm criminals. Before the new rule went into effect, the General Accounting Office did a study of its likely effect. During the first six months of the Clinton Administration's ninety-day retention policy, there were 235 cases in which prohibited gun buyers erroneously cleared the NICS background checks and were allowed to buy guns. Because the records of these erroneous approvals had been retained, the FBI was able to discover the errors and retrieve the firearms. According to the GAO, had the twenty-four-hour record destruction rule been in effect during the period examined, 97 percent of the prohibited buyers would have evaded detection and retained their guns. Chances are, some of those people would have committed violent crimes with their guns.[287]

It is therefore disingenuous in the extreme to claim that the gun lobby supports enforcement. The NRA, for example, has worked very diligently to both oppose gun laws and to undermine the enforcement of laws and regulations relating to firearms.

Myth 33: Gun Control Doesn't Work; Chicago Has Very Strict Laws and a Huge Gun Violence Problem

Illinois's relatively strict gun laws and Chicago's high-profile gun violence problem are used to make the case that strict gun laws don't make a difference.

Fact Check: First, anyone can cherry-pick data and find examples of a small number of cities with strict gun laws and high rates of violence in an attempt to show that tougher gun laws don't make a difference. One can also show the opposite by pointing to places with lenient laws and high rates of violence. That is why it is important to look at the overall picture. When we do that and examine the states as a whole, we see that states with weaker laws tend to have higher rates of gun deaths. In a previous analysis, Tom Gabor found that the states with the weakest laws collectively had two and a half times the rate of gun mortality as the states with the toughest gun laws.[288]

According to the Giffords Law Center, Illinois has an A- ranking in its gun laws, behind states like California and New Jersey.[289] It is therefore among the second tier of states in terms of the strength of its laws. Chicago got its reputation for having some of the strictest gun laws in the nation from two laws that are no longer on the books: a handgun ban and a gun registry. The registry ended in 2013. In 2010, Chicago's handgun ban was struck down by a federal appeals court. Chicago has a serious gun violence problem in certain parts of the city; however, the city as a whole ranks nowhere near the top when a homicide rate is computed that takes population differences into account. There are cities with three times Chicago's murder rate.[290] Thus, the logic behind the claim that Chicago has incredibly strict gun laws and that the city as a whole has an enormous gun violence problem is incorrect.

With that said, there is no doubt that Chicago has a significant gun violence problem. Regardless of the strictness of the gun laws of Chicago and Illinois, the fact that the state next door, Indiana, has weak laws serves to undermine their stronger laws since guns can easily be trafficked across state lines. One can literally cross the street from Chicago to enter the state of Indiana, buy a gun from an unlicensed seller, and return to Illinois, where one would be required to purchase guns through a licensed dealer. This gets around Illinois' background check requirement. Researchers from the University of Chicago traced all new guns recovered from crimes between 2009 and 2013. They found that 60 percent of the guns used in Chicago crimes were traced to out-of-state gun dealers and 20 percent of those were from neighboring Indiana.[291] There is abundant evidence from across the country that there is a pipeline from states with weaker laws to those with tougher laws.

The porous borders separating states do not support any argument for abandoning gun laws. Rather, they make the case for national laws, including the need to establish one standard for licensing owners and for banning or tightening controls on weapons that enable mass shootings.

Therefore, Illinois does not have the toughest gun laws, and Chicago, while it has a significant gun violence problem, is not an outlier with regard to rates of violence. Also, the number of guns on the street in Chicago is not an indication of failing gun laws but reflects, in large part, the weak laws in neighboring states.

Myth 34: Gun Owners and Non-Owners Disagree on Every Form of Regulation

Many people believe that the divide in opinion between gun owners and non-owners is so great that we can never bridge it. This is a dangerous view because it presents an obstacle to moving forward and addressing gun violence. If the public is portrayed as evenly divided for and against gun law reforms, Americans may come to truly believe that trying to achieve change will be futile.

Fact Check: In fact, this is not the case at all. While certain groups that advocate for gun owners, such as the NRA, appear to be implacably opposed to anti-gun violence measures, their membership as a whole is often at odds with officials in these organizations. In 2012, pollster

Frank Luntz conducted a survey of close to a thousand self-identified gun owners, half of whom were members or lapsed members of the NRA.[292] Luntz's survey revealed broad support among NRA members and other gun owners for a number of measures designed to prevent gun violence:

- 87 percent of non-NRA gun owners and 74 percent of NRA gun owners supported the need to conduct a criminal background check on any individual buying a firearm.

- 74 percent of NRA members believed that concealed carry permits should only be granted to applicants who have completed gun safety training.

- 68 percent of NRA members believed that these permits should be granted only to those who do not have prior arrests for domestic violence.

- 63 percent of NRA members believed that concealed weapons permits should be granted only to applicants who are twenty-one years of age or older.

- 75 percent of NRA members believed that concealed weapons permits should be limited to those who have not committed any violent misdemeanors.

A 2018 survey conducted by researchers at Johns Hopkins University shows that gun owners and non-owners are not far apart in their support of a number of policies:[293]

- Universal background checks were supported by 85 percent of gun owners and 89 percent of non-owners.

- License suspension for gun dealers who cannot account for twenty or more guns in their inventory was supported by 82 percent of gun owners and 86 percent of non-owners.

- Higher safety training standards for concealed weapon permit holders were supported by 83 percent of gun owners and 85 percent of non-owners.

- Better reporting of mental health records for background checks was supported by 84 percent of both gun owners and non-owners.

- Gun prohibitions for individuals subject to temporary domestic violence restraining orders were supported by 77 percent of gun owners and 82 percent of non-owners.

- Extreme risk protection orders (also known as red flag laws) were supported by 75 percent of gun owners and 80 percent of non-owners.

While the Johns Hopkins survey also revealed significant differences in relation to nine out of twenty-four policies examined, it showed that over half of gun owners still favor the following policies to restrict or regulate firearms:

- Requiring that owners lock up guns in the home to prevent access by youth

- Requiring individuals to obtain a license from law enforcement prior to buying a gun

- Allowing cities to sue gun dealers that allow criminals to obtain guns

Contrary to the belief that the differences between gun owners and non-owners are irreconcilable, there are many policies that have majority support among both groups. Author Fred Guttenberg has engaged in many interviews and debates with people in both factions to find common ground. During an interview preceding Father's Day weekend, 2021, on MSNBC's *Morning Joe* with Joe Scarborough and former Congressman Joe Walsh, both self-proclaimed "gun guys," they discussed many areas they agreed upon to reduce gun violence while still respecting the rights of gun owners and the Second Amendment. This common ground can serve as a basis for legal reforms going forward.

Myth 35: Bans and Restrictions Don't Work Since Criminals Don't Obey the Law and Can Buy Guns on the Illegal Market

This belief expresses the same sentiment as the slogan, "If guns were outlawed, only outlaws will have guns." This is the view that gun laws do not stop criminals from owning guns because they will find the means to obtain guns illegally. According to this view, responsible gun owners will obey bans, get required permits, and handle guns safely, while criminals, who are the ones causing all the problems with guns, will ignore laws. Thus, those who oppose gun violence prevention laws in general believe that such laws do nothing to prevent the criminal element from illegally obtaining and misusing firearms while creating unnecessary hardship for the vast majority of owners, who in the view of gun proponents are responsible in any case without such laws.

Fact Check: This line of argument is not only bogus but dangerous, as it can literally lead to delegitimizing all laws. Along similar lines, one can argue that those who kill, rape, molest children, and commit other heinous crimes will find a way to do so regardless of the presence of laws prohibiting such conduct, so why have any laws? Gun owners tell us all the time: "I don't misuse guns, so why pass laws to make things more difficult for me?" Our response is: "Most people don't murder and rape, but you still need laws prohibiting these acts and they can't just be applied only to some people."

Two assumptions underlying this belief is that people are either all good or all bad and that good people do not need laws and bad people do not respond to them. Consider NRA executive Wayne LaPierre's depiction of criminals: "The truth is that our society is populated by an unknown number of genuine monsters—people so deranged, so evil, so possessed by voices and driven by demons that no sane person can possibly ever comprehend them. They walk among us every day."[294]

This portrait of criminals as deranged individuals describes an extremely small fraction of lawbreakers. In fact, there is a large body of research showing that many citizens break a wide range of laws. Even violence is not limited to a small subpopulation of "evil" or "deranged" individuals. For example, a significant proportion of violent conduct occurs within the context of intimate relationships. The National Violence Against Women Survey has found that nearly 25 percent of surveyed women have been raped and/or physically assaulted by a current or previous spouse, cohabiting partner, or date.[295] These assaults by partners on a significant percentage of American women are not being committed by a small fraction of American men.

LaPierre's view of criminals as monsters who cannot be redeemed suggests that nothing short of their removal from society for life can protect us from them. However, research on focused deterrence initiatives shows that laws can lead individuals to modify their behavior when the certainty and severity of punishment are sufficiently high.[296] While no law deters everyone, there is no evidence that laws have no deterrent effect at all. While not proof of a causal relationship, states with tougher gun laws have fewer gun deaths, suggesting that tougher laws can serve as a deterrent or obstacle to violence.

Many experiments and other studies on human behavior show that some people do respond to penalties that are imposed with sufficient certainty.[297] The truth is that most people do not fall into extreme camps of being totally law-abiding or lawbreaking. Most of us are somewhere in between, and, given the right set of incentives, opportunities, and lack of deterrence, an individual may violate the law.[298]

Since the Brady bill was enacted, millions of Americans have been denied the ability to purchase a gun from a licensed dealer. While many of these individuals might have purchased a gun in the private market, at least some of these individuals may not have succeeded in obtaining a gun, potentially preventing the use of a gun in a crime or suicide attempt. Guns obtained from traffickers (much like illegal drugs) may be more costly, and not everyone (think of teenagers committing school shootings) will have easy access to guns through such networks. Waiting periods, requiring permits to purchase guns, and other measures have been shown to be effective in reducing gun violence.

It is also important to point out that laws do not exist merely to *prevent* crime. Many crimes, such as the physical and sexual abuse of children, frequently go undetected and unreported. Nevertheless, we must denounce such behaviors in the strongest terms. The law therefore serves as an expression of society's revulsion toward or disapproval of certain acts and draws the line at what is unacceptable. In the same way, setting limits on who can buy guns and on which weapons can be possessed by civilians communicates that we care about the many victims of gun violence and that we have a respect for life. Isn't this the message we want to send to young people?

In addition, two-thirds of all gun deaths in the US are suicides. A further 700 or so gun deaths each year are unintentional. We assume that suicide and unintentional gun death victims are not the ones LaPierre and others view as "monsters." Just 15 percent of all gun homicides are felony-type killings that occur during the course of a rape, robbery, burglary, or other crime. If these are the bad guys to whom the gun lobby is referring, their murders account for less than 4 percent of all gun deaths.

Many people who commit violent crimes have no history of violence. Some people drift between lawbreaking and law-abiding behavior. A significant number of "responsible" gun owners are lawbreakers. Many perpetrators of domestic violence live otherwise normal lives until they murder a spouse or commit a mass shooting. At this time, we are still trying to understand the behavior of the mass shooter in Las Vegas, the perpetrator of the deadliest mass killing in US history, who had no major red flags in his background. The shooter at Orlando Pulse, site of the country's second deadliest mass shooting, was a concealed weapon permit holder and security guard before going on his rampage. People may also turn their lives around in a positive direction, as indicated by those who discontinue their lives of crime. Thus, the good guy/bad guy idea is a false dichotomy, and we cannot predict with precision the identity of the next shooter. This is where reasonable gun laws, such as the banning of weapons of war, can make a difference by making it more difficult for the unknown shooters of tomorrow to bring about mass casualty incidents and other harms with firearms.

Myth 36: Banning Firearms Is Futile When So Many Weapons Are Already in Civilian Hands

Given that there are over 400 million guns in the hands of Americans as well as millions of military-style weapons, there is the view that a ban on any category of firearms will have limited impact as we are already awash in guns.

Fact Check: This is a legitimate concern, since it is easier to regulate something that has just come on the market as opposed to a product a large number of people already possess. If we attempt to ban AR-15 style weapons, one option is to have a grandfather provision that leaves those already sold with the owners—a step that is likely to doom the legislation—or else millions of people must surrender these weapons. Getting people to give up weapons already in their possession inevitably creates resistance and noncompliance. For a law to be successful, one has to make a strong case that evokes wide agreement from the public, a system of enforcement must be established for those who do not comply, and there must be some form of buyback to compensate owners when weapons worth hundreds or even thousands of dollars are turned in.

Given the current political environment, there is no doubt that banning military-grade weapons (including certain semiautomatic pistols) that can be fed by high-capacity ammunition magazines is an enormous challenge. A strong argument must be made to justify the expenditure of public funds and political capital to achieve this objective. However, we believe that the harm produced by these weapons makes this effort worthwhile. Fred Guttenberg, coauthor of this book, knows only too well the devastation to families produced when these weapons are in the hands of unstable or violence-prone individuals. Studies have shown that when military-style weapons are used in a mass shooting about six times more people are shot on average than when conventional firearms are used.[299] Many of the deadliest mass shootings in US history have been carried out using these weapons: in Las Vegas; in Orlando and Parkland, Florida; Newtown, Connecticut; Sutherland Springs, Texas; Aurora, Colorado; and more. These devastating attacks result in a disproportionate loss of life, as well as social, psychological, and economic consequences to communities and the country; failing to act to prevent them is therefore not an option.

Australia responded by taking action in 1996 after the worst mass shooting in its history. The country has a strong gun lobby and a frontier history, and it primarily had state rather than national gun laws. Following the mass shooting, Australia banned semiautomatic long guns and external ammunition magazines and bought them back from the owners. It also adopted a stricter licensing system for owners. The country has seen just one single mass shooting in public since 1996.[300] Banning and buying back millions of guns and ammunition magazines is an enormous undertaking that will take years. However, we must start somewhere, and gradually the number of these banned weapons will be reduced. With a reduction in their numbers, the cost of buying firearms will increase on the illegal market and they will become less affordable and accessible to those who would use them to commit harm. Just like illegal drugs, these weapons will become more out of reach financially for the young men (such as the Aurora theater shooter) who perpetrate many mass killings.

Myth 37: Gun Laws Are a First Step to the Complete Disarmament of the Population (the Slippery Slope Argument)

It is often argued by gun rights advocates that they must hold the line against any gun law because these laws are a slippery slope ultimately leading to the confiscation of all firearms. This canard provides cover to the gun lobby, since they can always lean on it when they have little basis to oppose seemingly benign measures like universal background checks.

Fact Check: As shown in Chapter 2, laws regulating firearms have existed since the founding of this country, from the settlement of the Western frontier straight through to the present. At no time has a general disarmament taken place in the 240-year history of the United States. In the Revolutionary Period, guns could be seized for use by militias but not for disarmament. Today there are a growing number of state "red flag" laws that call for the surrender of guns by domestic abusers or others who would pose a danger to themselves or the public. The surrender of guns is subject to a court order and usually has a time frame after which the owner can petition to have his firearms returned. These laws are designed to protect the public when a specific person poses a danger and have nothing in common with disarming a population. While general disarmament never has never taken place, African Americans have been subjected to discriminatory laws and practices aiming to disarm them. This was especially the case in the South following the Civil War and took the form of laws that kept freedmen from possessing guns.[301]

While general disarmament has never occurred, even the possibility has now been reduced even further with the Supreme Court's *Heller* decision of 2008. Departing from previous higher court rulings, this decision for the first time affirmed the right of individuals to keep arms in their homes for protection unless the potential owners are in a prohibited category such as convicted felons or the mentally ill. Therefore, any attempt at confiscating firearms would be a violation of the Second Amendment according to the most recent rulings.

In fact, the momentum seems to be tilting in the opposite direction as many major laws have been passed in the states to loosen gun laws over the last thirty or more years. Most states now make it a right to carry a weapon, and a person cannot be denied that right unless he or she falls in a prohibited category (e.g., has a felony record, has been diagnosed with mental health conditions leading to violence, or has been dishonorably discharged from the military). Most states allow the open carrying of a firearm. More than half the states now have a version of a Stand Your Ground (or Shoot First) law, which allows people to use lethal force when they feel threatened, with no duty to retreat.[302] The legal carrying of guns without a permit or training currently exists in twenty-five states, and this trend is spreading to additional states. All but a few states have some version of preemption laws expressly preventing local authorities from passing their own gun laws.

Even if we accepted the fantasy that the government wishes to confiscate all firearms, they would have to deal with about 400 million of them with no way of knowing who the owners are and how many guns each owner has. This is because there is no national registry of guns or owners. In fact, maintaining such a registry using the National Instant Background Check System would be a violation of federal law. Thus, staying with this fantasy, people would simply refuse to comply with an order to give up their guns, hide them, or bury them in their backyards, and no one would have a clue as to how many guns, if any, each resident had. Again, it is important to emphasize that any such edict would violate current interpretations of the Second Amendment and would therefore be a nonstarter. The confiscation argument is used to manipulate gun owners so they will oppose any law that places even minor restrictions on gun use.

Finally, the number of guns being produced in the US and in the hands of civilians hardly confers credibility to the argument that guns are endangered in the US. The number of guns manufactured by domestic firms each year has tripled over the last twenty years, from 3.9 million firearms in 2000 to 11.3 million in 2020.[303] While the US population increased by 18 percent over this period, annual gun production rose by 250 percent. Many guns today are also assembled by users—including ghost guns. During those years, the estimated inventory of firearms held by Americans increased from 259 million to about 400 million, a 54 percent increase.[304] Thus, over the last two decades, domestic gun manufacturing and ownership exceeded by a wide margin the growth of the US population. These indicators show that access to guns in the US is increasing and demonstrate that there is no basis to the fear that guns are in any way endangered in this country.

Gun Laws and Gun Violence Prevention: The Bottom Line

- There are many gun violence prevention initiatives that do not involve law reforms or public funding. Law enforcement strategies, such as "hot spot" policing, are focused on improving the enforcement of crime without changes to laws. Community programs, like violence interruption, focus on preventing the continuation of a cycle of violence among small groups. Citizen-based initiatives use volunteers and involve little or no public sector funds. These include educational programs to convince people to lock up their guns, gun buybacks, and consumer and investor activism, as well as funding and voting for candidates with clear anti-gun-violence platforms.

- Switzerland and Israel are often used by gun rights advocates as examples of two countries with permissive gun laws and low levels of violence. In fact, they both have strict gun laws and most of the firearms in these countries are connected to military service. The claim that Switzerland and Israel have higher levels of gun ownership and weaker gun laws than the US is untrue. Guns in both countries are far more tightly regulated than in the US, and both countries have much lower levels of gun violence than the US. Therefore, there is no basis to the argument that these countries somehow demonstrate that more guns lead to less crime.

- The statement that the Nazi rise to power was enabled by the disarmament of the German people is false. Hitler's regime actually loosened gun controls with the exception of restrictions on the Jewish population (less than 1 percent of the population). There was no general disarmament in Nazi Germany, yet still the country did not rise up against tyranny. In general, armed individuals are no match for a militaristic regime supported by a sophisticated national police force and a large army.

- Opponents of gun regulation, including the gun lobby, have argued that we need better enforcement of gun laws rather than new laws. This approach makes it appear as though they support effective enforcement and that we are facing a deluge of gun regulations. In fact, many gun law changes in recent years weakened gun controls and expanded gun rights; these legal changes included concealed carry laws, Stand Your Ground laws, and reductions in oversight of gun dealers. In addition, the gun lobby and its allies have vigorously opposed many basic controls on gun ownership, such as universal background checks and restrictions or bans on military-style weapons. The NRA has also vigorously opposed measures that would enable the identification and punishment of gun dealerships that promote gun trafficking.

- The argument that Chicago has the strictest gun laws and the highest levels of gun violence among US cities is false. While Chicago does have a significant gun violence problem, Chicago and Illinois' gun laws cannot be blamed since most crime guns come from states with weaker laws, such as Indiana. Illinois does not have the strictest gun laws, and Chicago is far from being the most violent city in America, contrary to impressions gained from the media. That aside, the challenges of implementing gun laws effectively in cities or states are well known as prohibited individuals can obtain guns in neighboring states with weaker laws. This situation does not doom state gun laws but complicates their successful implementation. It is therefore no reason to abandon gun laws but raises the question of abandoning the patchwork quilt of state laws in favor of some national laws, including the licensing of gun owners. If the entire country requires all gun owners to obtain a license and to undergo a rigorous screening process, one can no longer get around tougher laws by simply traveling across state lines.

- Many people believe that the divide in opinion between gun owners and non-owners is irreconcilable. This is a dangerous view because it can lead to the belief that efforts to tackle gun violence are futile. In fact, surveys show that by wide majorities, both gun owners and non-owners support a number of anti-violence measures, such as universal background checks, higher safety training standards for concealed weapon permit holders, extreme risk protection orders (known as red flag laws), and improved reporting of mental health records for background checks.

- The argument that gun laws are ineffective against criminals is bogus and dangerous, since this argument can be made in relation to any law. No law is effective against all perpetrators, but this is not an argument for abandoning laws that may modify the behavior of some individuals. Studies show that some gun laws can be effective and that states with tougher gun laws tend to have lower rates of gun mortality. There is also no clear division between criminals and the rest of society. Many people who commit homicides or mass shootings had no prior criminal record. They were "good guys" until the day of the shooting. Focusing on gun laws, such as assault weapon and high-capacity magazine bans, can aim to keep the most dangerous firearms out of the hands of all civilians.

- Military-style firearms like the AR-15 have been the weapons of choice in most of the worst mass shootings in the US. While it is challenging to remove such weapons from the marketplace, Australia has done so with great success, and it is imperative to do so because currently, large-scale massacres using these firearms are producing unacceptable levels of injuries and fatalities, increasing levels of fear and mistrust, and even posing a threat to the economy. A ban on those weapons that enable mass casualty incidents, along with smart messaging and compensation to owners, is the way forward. Over time, without a broad market, these weapons will be costly and difficult to acquire. High-capacity magazines also need to be banned since they have no role in civilian life other than to provide a means to commit mass murder.

- The argument that gun laws will eventually end in the confiscation of all guns is a red herring and is usually a sign that gun rights advocates have no substantive argument to make against a proposed gun law. Gun rights are alive and well in the US, as witnessed by the Supreme Court's *Heller* decision (which recognized for the first time an individual's right to gun ownership in 2008), the 2022 *Bruen* decision, and by the many state laws that have expanded gun rights over the last thirty or so years. There is no precedent for general disarmament in the US. Gun regulation has existed since the Revolutionary Period, and gun laws are more permissive today in many respects than in the past (e.g., concealed carry laws and Stand Your Ground laws). In addition, the quantity of guns manufactured and the number of guns held by civilians in the US are growing faster than the population, showing that guns are in no way endangered in the US.

Chapter 11

HOW TO COMBAT MISINFORMATION AND CHANGE THE FOCUS FROM GUN RIGHTS TO PUBLIC SAFETY

Misinformation ("fake news") is sowing increasing confusion in relation to politics and policy in many Western democracies. Online misinformation in particular poses an increasing risk to societies around the globe. For democracies to be effective, citizens must have access to accurate and objective information on political candidates and in relation to specific policy issues. Misinformation and disinformation (false information that is spread deliberately) contribute to cynicism and impede the ability of citizens to make sound political decisions. In 2019, more than eight in ten European citizens considered disinformation a concern in general and almost as many viewed it as a concern during pre-election periods.[305]

Beginning in the 1970s, psychologists showed that even after misinformation is corrected, false beliefs can persist.[306] Misinformation on COVID-19 has had such an impact that that even some patients dying from the disease still maintain that the pandemic is a hoax. Such falsehoods have influenced attitudes and behaviors around mask-wearing and vaccine uptake, creating an ongoing impediment to getting the virus under control. In the political domain, misinformation has been found to produce declining trust in mainstream media[307] and likely impacts voting behavior. Misinformation can even instigate violence, as in the case of the conspiracy theorist who fired a gun inside a Washington, DC, pizzeria in 2016. The Pizzagate conspiracy theory alleged that high-ranking members of the Democratic Party were engaged in child sex trafficking out of establishments like the pizza shop where the shooting occurred.

As Stephan Lewandowsky, a professor of psychology at the University of Bristol in the United Kingdom, notes, "The fundamental problem with misinformation is that once people have heard it, they tend to believe and act on it, even after it's been corrected."[308] This is because the misinformation may be consistent with a bias a person has.

From our numerous speaking engagements, we have learned that members of the public would be even more supportive of basic policies to prevent gun violence if they were better informed about laws and practices throughout America. For example, many people are surprised to hear that most Americans are not gun owners and are not a part of any form of "gun culture." They are struck by the fact that a small fraction of the population—superowners—own about half of the nation's guns. They are astounded by the fact that the gun lobby's influence on Congress has made guns exempt from basic consumer protections that are extended to toys, mattresses, hair dryers, and virtually every other consumer product and that the industry is shielded from liability when guns do what they are designed to do—kill humans, often more than one person at a time.

The recognition of these facts increases outrage and is also empowering, since the passivity of the American public on this issue is fueled by the mistaken belief that the gun lobby and the gun-owning segment of the population are politically all-powerful. Facts therefore matter, as they can challenge the common wisdom and can spur people to action. They can both motivate the uncommitted and increase the enthusiasm of those who are already on board with regard to the need to enact gun legislation and implement polices that will reduce our nation's levels of gun violence.

Identifying Leading Areas and Sources of Misinformation on Guns and Gun Violence

An initial step in combatting false information is to identify it and the sources that may be responsible for much of it. To identify misinformation, we must be aware of basic truths that are revealed through sound research. This task is in part fulfilled by this book. The purpose of creating this book was to use scientific evidence to counter leading myths promoted by the gun lobby and individuals who perpetuate the notion that guns are the path to freedom and safety in America. The primary aim of this book is not just to identify leading myths but to educate readers and to provide activists with talking points when they are interviewed, are lobbying for change, or are otherwise in debates with those spouting misinformation. Many of the myths discussed paralyze our ability to achieve change.

For example, the myth that gun laws are a recent development normalizes laws that are being passed by an increasing number of states to allow gun carrying without permits or training. That myth promotes the notion that America is returning to its gun-friendly roots, whereas, in reality, gun regulations were strict during the Revolutionary Period as well as in many frontier towns. Another myth is that gun violence is primarily a problem of the inner cities, thereby removing the necessity of passing laws applying to most of the country. The myths that there are more defensive gun uses than criminal ones or that most gun carriers have sufficient training to effectively use guns in a combat situation promotes the ideas of arming more citizens and of dispensing with permits and training for those carrying guns. Debunking such myths sheds light on arguments that have stood in the way of the adoption of basic, reasonable prevention measures like those enacted in other advanced countries.

Identifying sources of misinformation or disinformation is also critical so they can be called out for their falsehoods. While many false statements are made by individuals on social media and elsewhere every day, a few organizations are likely responsible for a disproportionate number of them. In our view, the National Rifle Association has waged a disinformation campaign for over thirty years, making the case for arming Americans based on the false notion that guns in the home and gun carrying promotes our collective safety and freedoms. The NRA has also promoted a distorted view of the Second Amendment, one that a former Chief Justice of the Supreme Court, Warren Burger—a conservative—called "one of the greatest pieces of fraud...on the American public."[309]

Most of the organization's "evidence" takes the form of bumper sticker type slogans such as, "Guns don't kill people, people kill people," "When you outlaw guns, only outlaws will have guns," "An armed society is a polite society," and, "The only way to stop a bad guy with a gun is with a good guy with a gun."

The NRA has also funded a body of scholarship to buttress the interpretation of the Second Amendment they wish to promote. From 1888 to 1969, every single law review article on the Second Amendment held the view that it protected the right of states to form militias, rather than protecting an individual's right to a gun for his own defense. The first article taking the individual rights view appeared in 1960; this was followed by a sprinkling of scholarship over the next fifteen years or so. In the late 1970s, coinciding with the NRA's extremist turn, a number of attorneys and professors began to produce a high volume of law review submissions adopting the individual rights view. Many of these works were funded by the NRA. This explosion of scholarship argued that the traditional view of the Second Amendment shared by the courts and historians was wrong and that the "right to keep and bear arms" was an individual right rather than a collective right to form a militia.[310]

It is a daunting task to counter the disinformation pumped out by large organizations like the NRA, as well as the sea of misinformation circulating among the public. Partnerships are needed to take on falsehoods that go viral or that appear in influential publications, programs, videos, and social media. Effective partnerships ought to include citizens, activists, journalists, gun violence researchers, software specialists who can develop programs to flag misinformation, and social media platforms. Aside from debunking, disseminating factual information is an important aspect of building the population's resistance to falsehoods.

A critical step to stanching the deluge of misinformation is to halt its spread on social media platforms, but that requires industry buy-in, which has been slow. During the 2020 presidential election, Twitter flagged tweets that contained misleading information about election results, and in December of that year, Facebook announced that it would begin removing posts with false claims about COVID-19 vaccines.

Making Factual Information Widely Available

Evidence-based arguments, such as those made in this book as well as new facts emerging from research, not only must be identified but need to reach the widest possible audience in order to effectively debunk the myths that form a roadblock to change. Researchers and authors need to establish a social media presence and connect with other researchers, activists, and concerned citizens to spread evidence-based findings and arguments that make the case for gun policy reform. Letters to the editor and op-ed articles in national and local papers are effective means of amplifying messages. Media appearances and public speaking engagements are also critical to elevating the messages.

Another important vehicle for disseminating accurate information on gun violence is through public service announcements (PSAs). PSAs seek to raise awareness, educate the public, and/or urge people to undertake certain actions. Dynamic message signs on the roads, such as those urging drivers not to drink and drive or informing them of the number of deaths on a particular road, have been found by researchers to be promising. There is some indication that repeating the message frequently increases their effectiveness.[311] Combining PSAs and a brochure was found to be effective in getting drivers to slow down and shift lanes when an emergency vehicle was stopped on the side of the road.[312] An independent evaluation has found that the McGruff "Take a bite out of crime" campaign launched in 1979 has been successful in raising awareness—especially in relation to information about violence—and also in getting people to take specific preventive actions. The program was found to be extremely cost effective.[313]

Evaluations of PSAs offer hope for campaigns that might, for example, encourage gun owners to store their weapons safely. Safe storage of firearms has been found to be one of the most effective measures in reducing suicides and unintentional injuries and deaths, as well as violent assaults, at least to a limited degree.[314] Near Fenway Park in Boston, a large billboard logs the number of gun deaths in America since the massacre of children and staff at Sandy Hook Elementary School in Newtown, Connecticut. Aside from logging overall deaths, billboards can count the number of children shot or killed with a gun, followed by a statement encouraging people to lock up their guns. Billboards, videos, or announcements comparing gun deaths in the US with other countries can also be powerful because the comparison is so striking. We need to shout from the rooftops the extent to which the US compares so unfavorably with other advanced countries and how many US gun policies do not reflect the views of most Americans.

Inoculating People Against Misinformation

In the 1960s, American officials were concerned that captured soldiers might be brainwashed by enemy troops. Yale University social psychologist William McGuire reflected on how people could develop resistance to unwanted persuasion through a "vaccine for brainwash," or in other words a "psychological inoculation."[315] Psychological inoculation is thought to work like immunization against a disease. With traditional vaccines, a weakened dose of a virus triggers the production of antibodies, enabling the body to ward off future infection more easily. Similarly, a persuasion "vaccine" triggers a thought process akin to "mental antibodies," offering attitudinal resistance against future persuasion attempts.

Psychological inoculation relies on two main mechanisms: (1) forewarnings of an attack (e.g., misinformation) to motivate resistance by producing a sense of threat, and (2) a preemptive refutation of the attack to provide people with specific counterarguments when they encounter attempts to influence them.[316]

One approach to building resistance to misinformation is to debunk incorrect information after it has spread. However, it is thought that inoculating people against falsehoods before they are exposed is more effective—a strategy known as "prebunking." This is achieved by warning people that a specific item of information is false and explaining why a source might lie or be misinformed about it before they encounter the bogus information. As an example, following the 2016 US election, Facebook began to display a warning beneath disputed articles. In 2018, they replaced the warnings with more subtle measures, such as reducing the post's size, providing links to fact-checker articles, and ranking the article lower in the news feed.

Rather than combatting falsehoods one item at a time, it may be possible to build resistance against misinformation in general (i.e., to confer blanket protection).[317] Researchers at Cambridge University in England have sought to develop a general resistance to manipulation through the creation of several games in which players assume the role of a manipulator. For example, in *Bad News*, players pretend to be a fake news creator and learn to use six key misinformation tactics.[318] By becoming acquainted with these tactics, individuals are more likely to be aware of when they are being lied to or manipulated. It is a more active way of learning to resist misinformation than having someone else debunk material. Games such as *Bad News* equip players with the skills necessary to identify and argue against misinformation and to prevent harmful disinformation from going viral.

Another way to address misinformation is to encourage people to reflect on the veracity of claims they encounter. Gordon Pennycook of the University of Regina (Canada) and his colleagues found that a simple accuracy prompt increased participants' ability to distinguish between real and fake news. In an experiment, participants viewed some truthful and false headlines and were asked to rate whether they would share each item on social media. Participants in the experiment were also asked to rate the accuracy of each headline. These participants were found to share more accurate news content compared with participants in the control group. Pennycook and his colleagues concluded that a simple accuracy reminder at the beginning of the study nearly tripled the level of truth discernment observed in participants' subsequent sharing intentions.[319]

Technically, this book both "prebunks" and debunks misinformation. The title, the first chapter, and the fact that most of the book is devoted to combatting myths serves as a warning that misinformation abounds in relation to gun violence. It therefore alerts readers to attacks on the truth in this area. For readers who have not previously been exposed to the myths tackled in this book, both the warning of these attacks on truth and the specific content of the responses to the misinformation will serve as a form of prebunking. For those who have been exposed to some of the material, the debunking of each myth will serve as a form of "booster" in which their resistance to the misinformation will reinforce their views. As indicated above, our goal is not just to inform the naïve but to strengthen the commitment of more informed individuals to evidence-based information in this area.

It is important to be mindful of research indicating that people are more likely to accept misinformation that is easy to hear and read. Rebuttals to misinformation similarly must be succinct and accessible in the language used to address the general reader.[320]

The Use of Technology to Combat Misinformation

The volume of information today, whether true or false, is so massive that it cannot be analyzed quickly and accurately simply through reliance on fact-checking organizations. The enormous volumes of information in both traditional and social media means we must rely on information technologies rather than solely on traditional approaches to detect and analyze misinformation. Detecting misinformation is a cumbersome task requiring a specialized workforce with the skills to distinguish between false and real news. An automated tool for misinformation detection is therefore required.[321]

Since gun violence is a public health concern, the field of related data and communications requires an organization like the World Health Organization (WHO) or a national body like the CDC, to identify and work to mitigate misinformation. The WHO has become increasingly involved with the issue with the proliferation of false information and conspiracy theories during the COVID-19 pandemic. In the context of a disease, the WHO website states:

> *An infodemic is too much information including false or misleading information in digital and physical environments during a disease outbreak. It causes confusion and risk-taking behaviours that can harm health. It also leads to mistrust in health authorities and undermines the public health response. An infodemic can intensify or lengthen outbreaks when people are unsure about what they need to do to protect their health and the health of people around them. With growing digitization—an expansion of social media and Internet use—information can spread more rapidly. This can help to more quickly fill information voids but can also amplify harmful messages. Infodemic*

management is the systematic use of risk- and evidence-based analysis and approaches to manage the infodemic and reduce its impact on health behaviours during health emergencies.[322]

As indicated at the outset of this chapter, the proliferation of misinformation can also create confusion in relation to gun violence, hindering the adoption of policies that could keep communities safer. Misinformation about the Second Amendment, for example, can lead people to believe that virtually any law restricting guns violates the Constitution.

The work of the WHO in relation to the pandemic illustrates what can be done by an organization dedicated to dealing with misinformation on gun violence. The WHO's Information Network for Epidemics aims to provide access to timely, accurate, and easy-to-understand information on public health events and flareups from trusted sources. It has held global consultations with an interdisciplinary group of experts and many other participants in webinars on managing COVID-19 misinformation. The WHO is setting up partnerships to support an effective response to the infodemic—the flood of rapidly spreading inaccurate and misleading information—through the development of global resources to perform fact checks and provide misinformation management. The WHO has a team to address rumors through publications and via live interviews with experts on its website, social channels, and other media. It is also collaborating with social media and search engines (Facebook, Google, Twitter) to filter out false information and to promote accurate information derived from credible sources like the CDC. The WHO is connecting with influencers through platforms like Instagram and YouTube to help disseminate factual messages to their followers.

A detailed discussion of the technical detection and analysis of misinformation is beyond the scope of this book. Basically, this type of analysis may include a focus on human networks, machine learning (a subset of artificial intelligence which allows a machine to learn from past data), and data and text mining methods in misinformation detection. These technologies help researchers understand the spread of disinformation and misinformation and track down the sources of false narratives.

Misinformation detection can be pursued through knowledge-based methods that either conduct fact checks manually using expert knowledge or automatically by employing such fact extractors and news aggregators as EventRegistry. Such services continuously search the internet for news on different topics.[323] This approach has given rise to online services such as PolitiFact. Another option is to focus on style-based features of text that expose the underlying intention behind the news. Text containing misinformation is more likely to use informal language, contain more typographical errors, and include more emotional content (including profanity).[324] Also, misinformation spreaders form more dense networks when compared with those spreading accurate news. These are some of the features that automated text analyses use to flag misinformation.

Next Steps: Combatting Gun Violence Misinformation

Going forward, combatting misinformation involves the following activities:

- Leadership will be needed from a major organization, preferably a public health organization such as the CDC or the WHO. These organizations have expertise in relation to public health issues such as violence, and they have experience with tackling misinformation.

- Partnerships must be forged between the lead organization, gun violence and information technology experts, media organizations, and social media companies such as Facebook (Meta) and Twitter.

- Misinformation must be identified with the use of automated tools, as well as with the help of the public.

- Leading sources of misinformation on gun violence, such as the NRA, must be identified so they can be closely monitored and their narratives can be countered.

- An online publication that can be widely disseminated needs to be created to report on new research findings, warn people about false narratives, and debunk misinformation that is circulating.

In creating materials to address misinformation, it is important to be mindful of the work of Norbert Schwarz, a professor of psychology and marketing at the University of Southern California. Schwarz identified a number of criteria that people use to decide whether information is true, including compatibility with other known information, credibility of the source, the internal consistency of the information, and whether there is supporting evidence.[325] His work shows that people are more likely to accept misinformation as fact if it is easy to read and hear. It follows that debunking efforts must also be easily understood by the general reader.

Others have found that people are more likely to believe misinformation when they fail to carefully reflect on the material, whether or not it is consistent with their political views.[326] Inoculation efforts must therefore repeatedly encourage people to reflect on the veracity and credibility of the material they read or hear.

Asserting Our Right to Live by Combatting the Biggest Lie Relating to Guns

Perhaps the leading piece of misinformation in relation to gun violence is the belief by many Americans that the Second Amendment of the Constitution confers an absolute right on individuals to "keep and bear arms." For over 200 years, the courts interpreted the Second Amendment as a collective right of states to form a militia, rather than as an individual right to gun ownership. The US Supreme Court's *Heller* ruling in 2008 changed that, recognizing for the first time the right to possess a gun in the home for self-defense. Even that ruling, however, stressed that "the Second Amendment right is not unlimited. It is not a right to keep and carry any weapon whatsoever in any manner whatsoever and for whatever purpose."[327]

As indicated in Chapter 7, no rights are absolute, as even the freedom of speech has its limits. Federal and state laws place limits on who can possess firearms (e.g., those without felony records, a mental illness, or a dishonorable discharge from the military) and certain categories of firearms, such as automatic weapons, are strictly regulated.

The gun lobby's campaign to convince the general public, politicians, gun owners, and even the courts that Americans have a fundamental, personal right to keep arms has had a profound impact on public opinion and policy. We constantly hear leaders and activists advocating for change conceding the argument over rights to those standing in the way of constructive changes to gun laws in support of public safety. Leaders of organizations working to prevent gun violence often will tamp down the expectations of their audience by stating that they respect the Second Amendment, even though the overwhelming majority of court rulings have upheld legal reforms. Proposals, such as licensing of gun owners and assault weapons bans, have not been deemed to be in violation of the Second Amendment.

Therefore, it is time to stop the self-limiting statements that cede the rights-based debate to gun extremists. It is also time to assert the right of Americans to live and to enjoy their lives without the constant fear of having it extinguished in a second by someone wielding a gun. America's founding documents hold the right to life to be sacred. The Declaration of Independence characterized the right to life as an inalienable right. The Constitution's Fifth and Fourteenth Amendments state that no persons should be deprived of life without due process of law. A number of international agreements the US has signed or ratified hold the right to life to be sacred. For example, the Universal Declaration of Human Rights affirms that "Everyone has the right to life, liberty, and security of the person (Article 3)."

The affirmation of the right to life in more than one of America's founding documents, as well as in international covenants signed or ratified by the US, illustrates that this right should carry at least as much weight as the Second Amendment right, which, as previously mentioned, is a limited right that does not preclude laws protecting human life. Elsewhere, Tom Gabor, one of this book's authors, has published "A Declaration of the Right to Live Free from Gun Violence." This Declaration can be found in Appendix A of this book.

The Declaration affirms the right of Americans to be safe from violence and intimidation while at home or work, during leisure activities, while shopping or attending school or college, and while using public transportation, attending public meetings, or in a place of worship. This right to be free from violence and the constant threat posed by guns counters the fiction that the Second Amendment right is absolute and supersedes all other rights. Asserting the public's right to be safe from gun violence is a critical step in countering misinformation and unlocking our nation's ability to combat gun violence.

A DECLARATION OF THE RIGHT TO LIVE FREE FROM GUN VIOLENCE

We propose the following Declaration of the right of Americans to live free from gun violence.

Preamble

Whereas the United States is a signatory to the Universal Declaration of Human Rights, which affirms that "Everyone has the right to life, liberty, and the security of person."

Whereas Amnesty International has declared that the US government's refusal to pass gun control laws represents a violation of its citizens' right to live free from violence and fear;

Whereas the Declaration of Independence affirms the right to life, liberty, and the pursuit of happiness;

Whereas the US Constitution was established, in part, to "insure domestic Tranquility" and "promote the general Welfare,"

Whereas over 40,000 Americans die and close to 100,000 suffer injuries from gunshot wounds each year;

Whereas many more Americans are traumatized and otherwise burdened by gun violence as witnesses to violence, family members, and caregivers;

Whereas there is an average of over one civilian mass shooting a day in the United States;

Whereas mass shootings have occurred in schools, colleges, at nightclubs and concerts, in movie theaters, places of worship, airports, workplaces, shopping malls, and at many other sites;

Whereas gun violence imposes heavy financial costs on individuals, the justice system, and the medical system;

Whereas high levels of gun violence and mass shootings reduce personal freedoms as they lead to more physical searches, intensified policing and surveillance levels, and more records maintained on private citizens;

Whereas most citizens are not gun owners;

Whereas most Americans favor reasonable gun laws, such as universal background checks, bans on assault weapons and high-capacity magazines, and keeping guns from the mentally ill; and,

Whereas the US Supreme Court ruled in 2008 (*District of Columbia v. Heller*) that the Second Amendment right is not unlimited and does not extend to the carrying of concealed weapons, possession of firearms by felons and the mentally ill, the carrying of firearms in sensitive places (e.g., schools and government buildings), or the carrying of dangerous or unusual weapons.

Declaration

Therefore, this *Declaration* affirms that:

The People have the right to feel safe in their homes, at work, and in public spaces;

The People have the right to be in gun-free environments while in school and college;

The People have a First Amendment right to express their opinions on all subjects free of intimidation by citizens with guns, both at public gatherings and in educational environments;

The People have the right to move about, shop, work, and enjoy leisure activities in their communities without a fear of gun violence;

The People have the right to enjoy shows, sporting events, movies, and concerts without the presence of armed citizens with guns other than police;

The People have the right to use public transportation and to enter terminals without a fear of gun violence;

The People have the right to attend church, temples, mosques, and other places of worship without the presence of citizens with guns;

The People should be spared the harms, economic costs, and traumas associated with gun violence.

ACKNOWLEDGMENTS

This book represents a special collaboration of two individuals who have come to the heavy and challenging topic of gun violence from very differently places.

Tom would like to thank his wife Christene for her unflagging support and love. He is also grateful to the many people with whom he has exchanged views on gun violence, including those with very different perspectives on gun policy. He has learned a great deal from these exchanges.

Fred wishes to thank his wife Jennifer and his son Jesse. Simply put, he could not have gone forward from the murder of Jaime without their constant love and support. He would also like to thank all others who have stood by his side as he has pursued his mission to reduce gun violence.

We would also like to thank Mango Publishing and their editorial team for all their support and encouragement. They have been an absolute delight to work with. Thank you also to our agent, Howard Yoon, who worked with us on this important project, helping to ensure that it would be published and read by as many people as possible.

ENDNOTES

1   Senator Hiram Johnson, Speech in 1917, https://www.azquotes.com/author/25791-Hiram_Johnson.

2   Allen Rostron, "The Dickey Amendment on Federal Funding for Research on Gun Violence: A Dissection," *American Journal of Public Health* 108, no.7 (2018): 865, https://www.ncbi.nlm.nih.gov/pmc/articles/PMC5993413/.

3   William Wan, "Congressional Deal Could Fund Gun Violence Research for the First Time Since the 1990s," *Washington Post,* December 16, 2019, https://www.washingtonpost.com/health/2019/12/16/congressional-deal-could-fund-gun-violence-research-first-time-since-s/.

4   Shannon Bond, "How Alex Jones Helped Mainstream Conspiracy Theories Become Part of American Life," *NPR*, August 6, 2022, https://www.npr.org/2022/08/06/1115936712/how-alex-jones-helped-mainstream-conspiracy-theories-into-american-life.

5   Thomas Gabor, "The Right of Americans to be Protected from Gun Violence," *Washington University Journal of Law and Policy* 66, no. 1 (2021): 43, https://openscholarship.wustl.edu/cgi/viewcontent.cgi?article=2215&context=law_journal_law_policy.

6   Amnesty International, *In the Line of Fire* (2018), 5, https://www.amnestyusa.org/wp-content/uploads/2018/09/egv_exec_sum.pdf.

7   Associated Press, "Judge Overturns California's 32-Year Ban on Assault Weapons; Likens AR-15 to "Swiss Army Knife,"" January 7, 2021, https://www.thedenverchannel.com/news/national/judge-overturns-californias-32-year-ban-on-assault-weapons-likens-ar-15-to-swiss-army-knife.

8   Tom Diaz, *Making a Killing: The Business of Guns in America* (New York: The New Press, 2000), 191.

9   Gallup, "Guns," https://news.gallup.com/poll/1645/guns.aspx.

10 ABC News/Washington Post Poll. "Gun Control, Immigration and Politics, April 16, 2013, http://www.langerresearch.com/wp-content/uploads/1148a1GunsImmigrationandPolitics.pdf.

11 Michael Waldman, "How the NRA Rewrote the Second Amendment," *Politico Magazine,* May 19, 2014, http://www.politico.com/magazine/story/2014/05/nra-guns-second-amendment-106856.

12   Gary Langer, "Most Now Oppose an Assault Weapons Ban." *ABC News,* December 16, 2015, https://abcnews.go.com/Politics/now-oppose-assault-weapons-ban-doubts-stopping-lone/story?id=35778846.

13   Pew Research Center, "Amid a Series of Mass Shootings in the US, Gun Policy Remains Deeply Divisive," April 20, 2021, https://www.pewresearch.org/politics/2021/04/20/amid-a-series-of-mass-shootings-in-the-u-s-gun-policy-remains-deeply-divisive/.

14   Carroll Doherty, "A Public Opinion Trend That Matters," *Pew Research Center,* January 9, 2015, https://www.pewresearch.org/fact-tank/2015/01/09/a-public-opinion-trend-that-matters-priorities-for-gun-policy/.

15   Cathy Lynn Grossman, "Poll: Americans Fear Terrorism, Mass Shootings—and Often Muslims As Well," *USA Today,* December 10, 2015, https://www.usatoday.com/story/news/2015/12/10/religion-news-service-poll-terrorism-shootings-muslims/77101070/.

16   Philip Cook and Kristin Goss, *The Gun Debate: What Everyone Needs to Know* (New York: Oxford Press, 2014), 7.

17   20-843 *New York State Pistol and Rifle Association Inc. v. Bruen* (06/23/2022).

18   Garry Wills, *A Necessary Evil: A History of American Distrust of Government* (New York: Simon and Schuster; 1999).

19   Ray Billington, *Westward Expansion: A History of the American Frontier* (New York: Macmillan, 1974), 587.

20   Adam Winkler, *Gunfight: The Battle Over the Right to Bear Arms in America* (New York: W.W. Norton, 2013), 113.

21   Winkler, *Gunfight,* 13, 135, and 167.

22   Robert Spitzer, "Gun Law History in the United States and Second Amendment Rights," *Law and Contemporary Problems* 80, no. 2 (2017): 55, https://scholarship.law.duke.edu/cgi/viewcontent.cgi?article=4825&context=lcp; p.56.

23   Robert Spitzer, "Stand Your Ground Makes No Sense," *The New York Times,* May 4, 2015, https://www.nytimes.com/2015/05/04/opinion/stand-your-ground-makes-no-sense.html.

24   Michael Weisser, *Gun Myths* (Ware, MA: Tee Tee Press, 2021), 13.

25   Michael Scherer, "Fact Check: The Gun Registry Red Herring," *Time,* January 24, 2013, https://swampland.time.com/2013/01/24/fact-check-the-gun-registry-red-herring/.

26   Aaron Karp, *Estimating Global Civilian-Held Firearms Numbers* (Geneva: Small Arms Survey, 2018), https://www.smallarmssurvey.org/sites/default/files/resources/SAS-BP-Civilian-Firearms-Numbers.pdf.

27   Katherine Schaeffer, "Key Facts About Americans and Guns," *Pew Research Center,* September 13, 2021, https://www.pewresearch.org/fact-tank/2021/09/13/key-facts-about-americans-and-guns/.

28   Tom Smith and Jaesok Son, *Trends in Gun Ownership in the United States*
      (Chicago: National Opinion Research Center, 2015), https://www.norc.org/PDFs/
      GSS%20Reports/GSS_Trends%20in%20Gun%20Ownership_US_1972-2014.pdf.

29   Smith and Son, *Trends in Gun Ownership in the United States*.

30   Sara Goo, "Why Own a Gun? Protection is Now Top Reason," *Pew Research Center*,
      May 9, 2013, https://www.pewresearch.org/fact-tank/2013/05/09/why-own-a-gun-
      protection-is-now-top-reason/.

31   Rachael Calcutt et al., "Effect of Mass Shootings on Gun Sales—A 20-year
      Perspective," *Journal of Trauma and Acute Care Surgery* 87, no. 3 (2019): 531.

32   BBC News, "America's gun culture—in seven charts," April 22, 2022, https://www.
      bbc.com/news/world-us-canada-41488081.

33   Schaeffer, "Key Facts about Americans and Guns."

34   Kim Parker et al., "The Demographics of Gun Ownership," *Pew Research Center*,
      June 22, 2017, https://www.pewresearch.org/social-trends/2017/06/22/the-
      demographics-of-gun-ownership/.

35   Rand Corporation, *Gun Ownership in America*, https://www.rand.org/research/
      gun-policy/gun-ownership.html.

36   Parker et al., "The Demographics of Gun Ownership."

37   Christopher Ingraham, "Three Million Americans Carry Loaded Handguns with
      Them Every Single Day, Study Says," *Washington Post*, October 19, 2017, https://
      www.washingtonpost.com/news/wonk/wp/2017/10/19/3-million-americans-carry-
      loaded-handguns-with-them-every-single-day-study-finds/.

38   Doherty, "A Public Opinion Trend that Matters."

39   Kim Parker et al., "Views on Gun Policy," *Pew Research Center*, June 22, 2017,
      https://www.pewresearch.org/social-trends/2017/06/22/views-on-gun-policy/.

40   Chris Jackson, Mallory Newall, and Charlie Rolason, "Three in Five Americans
      Disapprove of Biden's Handling of Economic Recovery," *Ipsos*, June 5, 2022,
      https://www.ipsos.com/en-us/news-polls/three-in-five-americans-disapprove-of-
      bidens-handling-of-economic-recovery.

41   Allison Brennan, "Analysis: Fewer US Gun Owners Own More Guns," *CNN*, July 31,
      2012, https://www.cnn.com/2012/07/31/politics/gun-ownership-declining/index.
      html.

42   Victor Agbafe, "The Vast Majority of Americans Support Universal Background
      Checks. Why Doesn't Congress?" *Harvard Kennedy School Institute of Politics*,
      https://iop.harvard.edu/get-involved/harvard-political-review/vast-majority-
      americans-support-universal-background-checks.

43   Christina Wilkie and Sam Stein, "NRA Supported Universal Background Checks
      After Columbine Massacre," *Huffington Post*, January 31, 2013, https://www.
      huffpost.com/entry/nra-gun-show-loophole_n_2593937.

44   David Hemenway, Deborah Azrael, and Matthew Miller, "National Attitudes
      Concerning Gun Carrying in the United States," *Injury Prevention* 7, (2001): 282,
      https://injuryprevention.bmj.com/content/injuryprev/7/4/282.full.pdf.

45   Thomas Gabor, *Confronting Gun Violence in America* (London: Palgrave Macmillan, 2016), 224.

46   Gabor, *Confronting Gun Violence in America*, Chap. 13.

47   Karp, *Estimating Global Civilian-Held Firearms Numbers*.

48   Erin Grinshteyn and D. Hemenway, "Violent Death Rates in the US Compared to Those of the Other High-Income Countries, 2015," *Preventive Medicine*, 123, (2019): 20, https://pubmed.ncbi.nlm.nih.gov/30817955/.

49   National Institute of Child Health and Human Development, Preventing Gun Violence, the Leading Cause of Childhood Death, National Institutes of Health, July 5, 2022, https://www.nichd.nih.gov/about/org/od/directors_corner/prev_updates/gun-violence-July2022.

50   Pierre Thomas et al., "Living with Gun Violence as Shootings Across US Continue to Rise," *ABC News*, November 9, 2021, https://abcnews.go.com/US/living-gun-violence-shootings-us-continue-rise/story?id=80949362--klds.

51   Garen Wintemute, "Experiences of Violence In Daily Life Among Adults in California: A Population-Representative Survey," *Injury Epidemiology* 9, no. 1 (2022), https://injepijournal.biomedcentral.com/articles/10.1186/s40621-021-00367-1?utm.

52   Matthew Miller et al., "Road Rage in Arizona: Armed and Dangerous?" *Accident Analysis and Prevention* 34, no. 6 (2002): 807.

53   David Hemenway et al., "Is an Armed Society a Polite Society? Guns and Road Rage," *Accident Analysis and Prevention* 38, no. 4 (2006): 687.

54   FBI, *Police Employee Data*, https://ucr.fbi.gov/crime-in-the-u.s/2011/crime-in-the-u.s.-2011/police-employee-data.

55   David Hemenway and Sara Solnick, "The Epidemiology of Self-Defense Gun Use: Evidence from the National Crime Victimization Surveys 2007-2011," *Preventive Medicine 79* (2015): 22.

56   FBI, *A Study of Active Shooter Incidents in the United States Between 2000 and 2013* (US Department of Justice, 2013, 11), https://www.fbi.gov/file-repository/active-shooter-study-2000-2013-1.pdf/view.

57   David Hemenway and Deborah Azrael, "The Relative Frequency of Offensive and Defensive Gun Use: Results of a National Survey," *Violence and Victims* 15 (2000): 257.

58   Thomas Gabor, *CARNAGE: Preventing Mass Shootings in America* (St. Petersburg, FL: BookLocker, 2021).

59   David Swedler et al., "Firearm Prevalence and Homicides of Law Enforcement Officers in the United States," *American Journal of Public Health* 105, no. 10 (2015): 2042.

60   Franklin. Zimring, *When Police Kill* (Cambridge, MA: Harvard University Press, 2017), 70.

61   Zimring, *When Police Kill*, Chapter 4.

62   Zimring, 79.

63   Zimring, 57, 62.

64   Kerry Shaw and Norm Stamper, "I Ran a Big City Police Department. The Way We Train Cops to Use Lethal Force is Broken," *The Trace*, July 12, 2016, https://www.thetrace.org/2016/07/seattle-former-top-cop-guns-america-policing-problem/.

65   CDC, "All Injuries," National Center for Health Statistics, https://www.cdc.gov/nchs/fastats/injury.htm.

66   Brady, "Key Statistics," https://www.bradyunited.org/key-statistics.

67   Chelsea Bailey, "More Americans Killed by Guns Since 1968 Than in All US Wars–Combined," *NBC News*, October 4, 2017, https://www.nbcnews.com/storyline/las-vegas-shooting/more-americans-killed-guns-1968-all-u-s-wars-combined-n807156.

68   National Institute of Justice, *Gun Violence in America*, February 26, 2019, https://nij.ojp.gov/topics/articles/gun-violence-america.

69   Susan Sorenson and Rebecca Schut, "Nonfatal Gun Use in Intimate Partner Violence: A Systematic Review of the Literature," *Trauma, Violence and Abuse* 19, no. 4 (2016), https://journals.sagepub.com/doi/abs/10.1177/1524838016668589.

70   Fran Norris, "Impact of Mass Shootings on Survivors, Families and Communities," *PTSD Research Quarterly* 18, no. 3 (2007): 1.

71   American Psychological Association, *Stress in America: Generation Z*, 2018, https://www.apa.org/news/press/releases/stress/2018/stress-gen-z.pdf.

72   Morning Consult, *How 2020 is Impacting Gen Z's Worldview*, https://morningconsult.com/form/gen-z-worldview-tracker/

73   Jamie Ducharme, "A Third of Americans Avoid Certain Places Because They Fear Mass Shootings," *Time*, August 15, 2019, https://time.com/5653218/massshootings-stress/.

74   World Health Organization, *Self-Directed Violence*, https://www.who.int/violence_injury_prevention/violence/world_report/factsheets/en/selfdirectedviolfacts.pdf.

75   Kay Jamison, *Night Falls Fast: Understanding Suicide* (New York: Knopf, 1999), 47.

76   Grinshteyn and Hemenway, "Violent Death Rates in the US Compared to Those of the Other High-Income Countries, 2015."

77   Douglas Wiebe, "Homicide and Suicide Risks Associated with Firearms in the Home: A National Case-Control Study," *Annals of Emergency Medicine* 41, no. 6 (2003): 775.

78   David Studdert et al., "Homicide Deaths Among Adult Cohabitants of Handgun Owners in California, 2004 to 2016: A Cohort Study," *Annals of Internal Medicine*, (2022), https://www.acpjournals.org/doi/10.7326/M21-3762?utm.

79   Jacquelyn Campbell et al., "Risk Factors for Femicide in Abusive Relationships: Results from a Multisite Case Control Study," *American Journal of Public Health* 93, no. 7 (2003): 1089, https://www.ncbi.nlm.nih.gov/pmc/articles/PMC1447915/.

80   Violence Policy Center, *Firearm Justifiable Homicides and Non-Fatal Self-Defense Gun Use*. Washington, DC: 2019, https://vpc.org/studies/justifiable19.pdf.

81   Matthew Miller, Deborah Azrael, and David Hemenway, "Firearm Availability and
     Suicide, Homicide, and Unintentional Firearm Deaths Among Women," *Journal
     of Urban Health* 79, no. 1 (2002): 26, https://www.ncbi.nlm.nih.gov/pmc/articles/
     PMC3456383/.

82   Kevin M. Grassel et al., "Association between Handgun Purchase and Mortality
     from Firearm Injury," *Injury Prevention* 9 (2003): 50.

83   Sorenson and Schut, Non-Fatal Gun Use in Intimate Partner Violence.

84   Evan Defilippis, "Having a Gun in the House Doesn't Make a Woman Safer,"
     The Atlantic, February 23, 2014, https://www.theatlantic.com/national/
     archive/2014/02/having-a-gun-in-the-house-doesnt-make-a-woman-
     safer/284022/.

85   Schaeffer, "Key Facts About Americans and Guns."

86   FBI, *Active Shooter Incidents: 20-Year Review, 2000-2019,* 7. https://
     schoolsafetyresources.nh.gov/wp-content/uploads/2021/06/active-shooter-
     incidents-20-year-review-2000-2019-060121.pdf.

87   Gerrard Kaonga, "Uvalde Shooting Video Unedited: What 77-Minute Hallway
     Video Reveals," *Newsweek*, July 13, 2022, https://www.newsweek.com/uvalde-
     shooting-footage-unedited-police-robb-elementary-school-texas-security-hallway-
     camera-1724126.

88   Kate Stringer, "Gallup Poll: Most Educators Don't Want to Be Armed with Guns.
     The74, March 16, 2018, https://www.the74million.org/gallup-poll-most-educators-
     dont-want-to-be-armed-with-guns.

89   National Center for Education Statistics, *Fast Facts,* https://nces.ed.gov/fastfacts/
     display.asp?id=28.

90   Tim Walker, "Out of My Pocket: Educators Speak Out on Buying Their Own Schools
     Supplies," *NeaToday,* September 14, 2018, https://www.nea.org/advocating-for-
     change/new-from-nea/outofmypocket-educators-speak-out-buying-their-own-
     school.

91   Michael Hiltzik, "One Big Problem With the Idea of Arming Teachers: Insurance
     Companies Won't Play Along and With Good Reason," *Los Angeles Times,*
     February 26, 2018, http://www.latimes.com/business/hiltzik/la-fi-hiltzik-arming-
     teachers-20180226-story.html.

92   Marissa Martinez, "Arming Teachers Only Creates More Problems," *The Daily
     Northwestern*, February 25, 2018, https://dailynorthwestern.com/2018/02/25/
     lateststories/martinez-arming-teachers-creates-problems/.

93   AP, "More Than 30 Mishaps From Armed Adults at Schools," *CBS News,* May
     6, 2018, https://www.cbsnews.com/news/armed-adults-schools-mishaps-
     analysis-2018-05-06.

94   AP, More Than 30 Mishaps from Armed Adults at Schools.

95   SurveyUsa, *Survey on Behalf of Everytown for Gun Safety,* December, 2018, https://
     www.surveyusa.com/client/PollReport.aspx?g=4a9eed40-c8b0-419c-ae82-
     71e1dbd19ca0&c=254.

96   FBI, *Crime in the United States, 2017,* Table 16, https://ucr.fbi.gov/crime-in-the-
      u.s/2017/crime-in-the-u.s.-2017/tables/table-16.

97   Iowa Community Indicators Program, *Urban Percentage of the Population for
      States, Historical,* Iowa State University, https://www.icip.iastate.edu/tables/
      population/urban-pct-states.

98   National Center for Health Statistics, Firearm mortality by state. Centers for Disease
      Control and Prevention. Available at: https://www.cdc.gov/nchs/pressroom/
      sosmap/firearm_mortality/firearm.htm.

99   David Correa and Nick Wilson, Gun Violence in Rural America, The Center for
      American Progress, September 26, 2022, https://www.americanprogress.org/
      article/gun-violence-in-rural-america.

100   Rand, Gun Ownership in America. Available at: https://www.rand.org/research/
      gun-policy/gun-ownership.html.

101   Gabor, *Confronting Gun Violence in America,* 123-126.

102   Melissa Chan, "Gun-Makers Tell Congress Mass Shootings are a "Local" Problem
      Not Caused by "Inanimate" Firearms," *NBC* News, July 27, 2022, https://www.
      nbcnews.com/politics/politics-news/gun-makers-tell-congress-mass-shootings-
      are-local-problem-not-caused-i-rcna40256.

103   Michael Weisser, "Want to Go to the NRA Show?" https://mikethegunguy.
      social/2022/03/17/want-to-go-to-the-nra-show/.

104   Dennis Henigan, *Lethal Logic: Exploding the Myths that Paralyze American Gun
      Policy* (Washington, DC: Potomac Books, 2009), 31.

105   Arthur Kellermann et al., "The Epidemiologic Basis for the Prevention of Firearm
      Injuries," *Annual Review of Public Health* 12 (1991): 17.

106   R. Richter and M. Zaki, "Selective Conservative Management of Penetrating
      Abdominal Wounds," *Annals of Surgery* 166, no. 2 (1967): 238.

107   Philip Cook, "Robbery Violence," *Journal of Criminal Law and Criminology* 78, no. 2
      (1987): 357.

108   Thomas Gabor et al., *Armed Robbery* (Springfield, IL: Charles Thomas, 1987, 103-
      104.

109   Franklin Zimring, "Is Gun Control Likely to Reduce Violent Killings?" *University of
      Chicago Law Review* 35, no. 4 (1968): 721.

110   Josh Sugarmann, *Every Handgun Is Aimed at You* (New York: The New Press, 2001),
      156.

111   Bryn Caswell, "Dayton Police Chief Richard Biehl Presents at US Secret Service
      Mass Attack Seminar," *Dayton Now,* August 6, 2020, https://dayton247now.com/
      news/local/dayton-police-chief-richard-biehl-presents-at-us-secret-service-mass-
      attack-decision.

112   National Law Enforcement Memorial Fund, *2021 End of Year Preliminary
      Law Enforcement Officers Fatalities Report,* https://nleomf.org/wp-content/
      uploads/2022/01/2021-EOY-Fatality-Report-Final-web.pdf.

113   Philip Cook, "The Effect of Gun Availability on Violent Crime Patterns," *Annals of the American Academy of Political and Social Science* 455, no. 1 (1981): 63.

114   Gary Kleck and Karen McElrath, "The Effects of Weaponry on Human Violence," *Social Forces* 69, no. 3 (1991): 669.

115   Shira Kantor, "Sniper Killings Grip Maryland," *Chicago Tribune*, October 4, 2002, http://articles.chicagotribune.com/2002-10-04/news/0210040287_1_shootings-dealership-al-briggs.

116   Justin Sayers, "Phoenix Freeway Shootings: What You Need to Know," *The Arizona Republic*, September 25,2015, http://www.azcentral.com/story/news/local/phoenix/breaking/2015/09/10/phoenix-freewayshootings-what-you-need-know/72029778/.

117   Michael Martinez et al., "Albuquerque Road Rage: Man in Custody After 4-Year-Old Shot, Killed," *CNN.com*, October 21, 2015, http://www.cnn.com/2015/10/21/us/child-road-ragedeath/index.html.

118   Stephanie Allen, "Innocent Bystander Shot While Driving on OBT, Cops Say," *Orlando Sentinel,* September 14, 2015, http://www.orlandosentinel.com/news/breaking-news/os-shooting-stolen-vehicle-obt-408-20150914-story.html.

119   Linda Saltzman et al., "Weapon Involvement and Injury Outcomes in Family and Intimate Assaults," *Journal of the American Medical Association* 267, no. 22 (1992): 3043.

120   Leonard Berkowitz and Anthony LePage, "Weapons as Aggression-Eliciting Stimuli," *Journal of Personality and Social Psychology* 7, no. 2 (1967): 202.

121   Jennifer Klinesmith, Tim Kasser, and Francis McAndrew, "Guns, Testosterone, and Aggression," *Psychological Science* 17, no. 7 (2006): 568.

122   GVPedia, *Facts About Firearms Policy Initiative*, 2021, 68.

123   Alex Yablon, "Bullets Per Body Rise as High-Capacity Magazines Gain Criminal Following," *The Trace*, January 2, 2018, https://www.thetrace.org/newsletter/chicago-multiple-gunshots-high-capacity-handguns/.

124   Greg Myre, "A Brief History of the AR-15," *NPR*, February 28,2018, https://www.npr.org/2018/02/28/588861820/a-brief-history-of-the-ar-15.

125   "Breaking: Jim Sullivan, AR-15 Designer, Makes Some Controversial Statements on HBO Tonight," (May 24, 2016), www.thefirearmblog.com/blog/2016/05/24/breaking-jim-sullivan-ar-15-designer-makes-some-controversial-claims-on-hbo-tonight.

126   Weisser, *Gun Myths*, 31.

127   Weisser, 34.

128   Weisser, 35-36.

129   Emily Shapiro, "Inside the Rise of AR-15-Style Rifles in America," *ABC News*, October 27, 2021, https://abcnews.go.com/US/inside-rise-ar-15-style-rifles-america/story?id=78842406.

130   David Hemenway, *Private Guns, Public Health* (Ann Arbor: University of Michigan Press, 2004), 72.

131 Everytown for Gun Safety, *The Impact of Gun Violence on Children and Teens*, December 28, 2021, https://everytownresearch.org/report/the-impact-of-gun-violence-on-children-and-teens/.

132 Gabor, *Confronting Gun Violence in America*, 8.

133 FBI, *2019 Crime in the US*, Tables 14 and 20 under homicide, https://ucr.fbi.gov/crime-in-the-u.s/2019/crime-in-the-u.s.-2019/tables/table-20; https://ucr.fbi.gov/crime-in-the-u.s/2019/crime-in-the-u.s.-2019/tables/expanded-homicide-data-table-14.xls.

134 Gun Violence Archive, *Past Summary Ledgers*, https://www.gunviolencearchive.org/past-tolls.

135 Elinore J. Kaufman et al., "Epidemiologic Trends in Fatal and Nonfatal Firearm Injuries in the US, 2009-2017," *JAMA Internal Medicine* 18, no. 2 (2021): 237, https://jamanetwork.com/journals/jamainternalmedicine/fullarticle/2773788.

136 David Hemenway and Sara Solnick, "The Epidemiology of Self-Defense Gun Use: Evidence from the National Crime Victimization Surveys, 2007-2011," *Preventive Medicine* 79 (2015): 22. https://www.sciencedirect.com/science/article/abs/pii/S0091743515001188

137 Michael Planty and Jennifer Truman, *Firearm Violence, 1993-2011* (Washington, DC: Bureau of Justice Statistics, 2013), https://bjs.ojp.gov/content/pub/pdf/fv9311.pdf.

138 Jennifer Mascia, "How often are guns used for self-defense?" *The Trace*, June 3, 2022, https://www.thetrace.org/2022/06/defensive-gun-use-data-good-guys-with-guns/?utm.

139 Arthur Kellermann et al., "Gun Ownership as a Risk Factor for Homicide in the Home," *New England Journal of Medicine* 329 (1993): 1084, https://www.nejm.org/doi/full/10.1056/NEJM199310073291506.

140 Arthur Kellermann et al., "Injuries and Deaths Due to Firearms in the Home," *Journal of Trauma* 45 (1998): 263, https://pubmed.ncbi.nlm.nih.gov/9715182/.

141 David Studdert, "Owning Guns Puts People in Your Home at Greater Risk of Being Killed, New Study Shows," Time, June 3, 2022, https://time.com/6183881/gun-ownership-risks-at-home/.

142 David Hemenway and Matthew Miller, "Gun Threats Against and Self-Defense Gun Use by California Adolescents," *Archives of Pediatric and Adolescent Medicine* 158, no. 4 (2004): 395, https://pubmed.ncbi.nlm.nih.gov/15066882/.

143 Hemenway and Miller, Gun Threats Against and Self-Defense Gun Use by California Adolescents, Abstract.

144 Gary Kleck and Mark Gertz, "Armed Resistance to Crime: The Prevalence and Nature of Self-Defense with a Gun," *Journal of Criminal Law and Criminology* 86 (1995): 150, https://scholarlycommons.law.northwestern.edu/cgi/viewcontent.cgi?article=6853&context=jclc.

145 Bureau of Justice Statistics, *National Crime Victimization Survey*, https://bjs.ojp.gov/data-collection/ncvs.

146 Hemenway, *Private Guns, Public Health*, 67.

147   Arthur Kellermann et al., "Weapon Involvement in Home Invasion Crimes," *Journal of the American Medical Association* 273 (1995): 1759.

148   Hemenway, *Private Guns, Public Health*, 67.

149   Philip Cook et al., "The Gun Debate's New Mythical Number: How Many Defensive Uses Per Year," *Journal of Policy Analysis and Management* 16 (1997): 463.

150   *District of Columbia et al. v. Heller* 554 U.S. 570 (2008). Supreme Court of the United States, http://www.supremecourt.gov/opinions/07pdf/07-290.pdf.

151   Robert Spitzer, "Stand Your Ground Makes No Sense," *The New York Times*, May 4, 2015, https://www.nytimes.com/2015/05/04/opinion/stand-your-ground-makes-no-sense.html.

152   Elise Schmelzer, "Good Samaritan in Olde Town Arvada Shooting Was Killed by Police, Source Says," *The Denver Post*, June 24, 2021, https://www.denverpost.com/2021/06/24/johnny-hurley-arvada-police-shooting/.

153   Molly Hennessey-Fiske, "Dallas Police Chief: Open Carry Makes Things Confusing During Mass Shootings," *Los Angeles Times*, July 11, 2016, https://www.latimes.com/nation/la-na-dallas-chief-20160711-snap-story.html.

154   Cate Cauguiran and Michelle Gallardo, "Illinois Police Officer Shoots Bouncer at Nightclub After He Takes Down Shooter, Witnesses Say," *ABC Eyewitness News*, November 11, 2018, https://abc11.com/robbins-shooting-bouncer-shot-jemel-roberson-mannys-blue-room/4680032/.

155   Jay Croft, "Philando Castile Shooting: Dashcam Video Shows Rapid Event," *CNN*, June 21, 2017, https://www.cnn.com/2017/06/20/us/philando-castile-shooting-dashcam/index.html.

156   Giffords Law Center, Concealed Carry, https://giffords.org/lawcenter/gun-laws/policy-areas/guns-in-public/concealed-carry/

157   John Lott, *More Guns, Less Crime* (Chicago: University of Chicago Press, 1998).

158   Abhay Aneja, John Donohue, and Alexandria Zhang, "The Impact of Right To Carry Laws and the NRC Report: Lessons for the Empirical Evaluation of Law and Policy," *American Law and Economy Review* 13, no. 2 (2011): 565.

159   Clifton Parker, "Right-To-Carry Gun Laws Linked to Increase in Violent Crime, Stanford Research Shows," *Stanford News*, November 14, 2014, https://news.stanford.edu/2014/11/14/donohue-guns-study-111414/.

160   John J. Donohue, Abhay Aneja and Kyle D. Weber, "Right-to-Carry Laws and Violent Crime: A Comprehensive Assessment Using Penal Data and a State-Level Synthetic Control Analysis," *Journal of Empirical Legal Studies* 16 (2019): 198.

161   Henigan, Lethal Logic, 133.

162   Philip Cook and Kristin Goss, *The Gun Debate: What Everyone Needs to Know* (New York,: Oxford University Press, 2014), 22.

163   David Fortunato, "Can Easing Concealed Carry Deter Crime?" *Social Science Quarterly* 96, no. 4 (2015): 1.

164   Paul Reeping et al., "State Gun Laws, Gun Ownership and Mass Shootings in the US: Cross-sectional Time Series," *British Medical Journal* 364 (2019): 1542, https://www.bmj.com/content/bmj/364/bmj.l542.full.pdf.

165   FBI, Active Shooter Incidents, 20-Year Review, 2000-2019, https://www.fbi.gov/file-repository/active-shooter-incidents-20-year-review-2000-2019-060121.pdf/view.

166   Louis Klarevas *Rampage Nation: Securing America from Mass Shootings* (New York: Prometheus, 2016), 169.

167   Thomas Gabor, *CARNAGE: Preventing Mass Shootings in America* (St. Petersburg, FL: Booklocker, 2021), 91.

168   Violence Policy Center, *Concealed Carry Killers*. Updated September, 2021, https://concealedcarrykillers.org/

169   Jennifer Mascia, "Are Road Rage Shootings Increasing?" *The Trace*, May 2, 2022, https://www.thetrace.org/2022/05/road-rage-shooting-gun-violence/?utm.

170   Michael Daly, "Gun Thefts Are Through the Roof Because Gun Nuts Won't Lock Their Cars," *The Daily Beast*, June 17, 2021, https://www.thedailybeast.com/gun-thefts-surge-with-criminals-shopping-for-firearms-in-unlocked-cars.

171   Giffords Law Center, *Concealed Carry,* https://giffords.org/lawcenter/gun-laws/policy-areas/guns-in-public/concealed-carry/.

172   Jennifer Mascia and Chip Brownlee, "31 States Let People Carry Guns Without Learning How to Shoot One," *The Trace*, January 25, 2022, https://www.thetrace.org/2022/01/which-states-require-firearm-safety-course-concealed-carry/?utm.

173   Giffords Law Center, *Concealed Carry in Delaware,* https://giffords.org/lawcenter/state-laws/concealed-carry-in-delaware/

174   Joseph Vince, Timothy Wolfe, and Layton Field. *Firearms Training and Self-Defense* (Chicago: National Gun Victims Action Council, 2015), 4.

175   Joshua Holland, "Tactical Experts Destroy the NRA's Heroic Gunslinger Fantasy," *The Nation*, October 5, 2015, https://www.thenation.com/article/archive/combat-vets-destroy-the-nras-heroic-gunslinger-fantasy/.

176   Holland, Tactical Experts Destroy the NRA's Gunslinger Fantasy.

177   Gregory Morrison, "Police Firearms Training Survey. Preliminary Findings," Paper presented at the Annual Meeting of the Academy of Criminal Justice Sciences. Anaheim, CA: March, 2002.

178   Weisser, *Gun Myths*, 39-40.

179   Personal communication, December 14, 2021.

180   J. Anderson, "Iowan who wanted to surprise dies in accidental shooting," *Omaha World-Herald*, June 12, 2002, 1A.

181   Associated Press, "Florida Woman Shoots Her 7-Year-Old Grandson, Mistaking Him for an Intruder in Her Home," *National Post*, August 19, 2014, https://nationalpost.com/news/florida-woman-shoots-her-seven-year-old-grandson-mistaking-him-for-an-intruder-in-her-home.

182   Vince et al., *Firearms Training and Self-Defense*, 19.

183   Giffords Law Center, Concealed Carry.

184   Thomas Gabor, *ENOUGH: Solving America's Gun Violence Crisis* (Lake Worth, FL: Center for the Study of Gun Violence, 2019), Chapter 2.

185   Megan O'Matz and John Maines, "License to Carry: A Sun-Sentinel Investigation," *Sun-Sentinel*, January 28, 2007, http://articles.sunsentinel.com/2007-01-28/news/0701270316_1_gun-licensing-system.

186   Susan Glick and Marty Langley, *License to Kill and Kidnap and Rape and Drive Drunk: An Update on Arrests of Texas Concealed Handgun License Holders* (Washington, DC: Violence Policy Center; 1999), 1.

187   Michael Luo, "Guns in Public, and Out of Sight," *New York Times*, December 26, 2011, https://www.nytimes.com/2011/12/27/us/more-concealed-guns-and-some-are-in-the-wrong-hands.html?pagewanted=all.

188   Violence Policy Center, *Concealed Carry Killers*.

189   "Sheriff: Chilling Confession In Lakeland Shooting Rampage," *baynews9.com*, September 8, 2021; "Polk Sheriff: 'Shooting Rampage' in Lakeland Left 4 Dead, Including a Baby," *baynews9.com*, September 5, 2021.

190   Liz Mineo, "The Loaded History of Self-Defense," *The Harvard Gazette*, March 7, 2017, https://news.harvard.edu/gazette/story/2017/03/the-loaded-history-of-self-defense/.

191   Kris Hundley, Susan Martin, and Connie Humburg, "Florida Stand Your Ground Law Yields Some Shocking Outcomes Depending on How Law is Applied," *Tampa Bay Times*, June 1, 2012, http://www.tampabay.com/news/publicsafety/crime/florida-stand-your-ground-law-yields-some-shockingoutcomes-depending-on/1233133.

192   Ben Montgomery and C. Jenkins, "Five Years Since Florida Enacted 'Stand Your Ground' Law, Justifiable Homicides Are Up," *Tampa Bay Times*, October 15, 2010, http:// www.tampabay.com/news/publicsafety/crime/five-years-since-florida-enacted-stand-your-groundlaw-justifiable/1128317.

193   David Humphreys, Antonio Gasparrini, Douglas Wiebe, "Evaluating the Impact of Florida's 'Stand Your Ground' Self-Defense Law on Homicide and Suicide by Firearm: An Interrupted Time Series Study," *JAMA Internal Medicine* 177 (2017): 44, https://www.ncbi.nlm.nih.gov/pubmed/27842169.

194   Chelsea Parsons, E Weigend, *The Devastating Impact of Stand Your Ground in Florida. Center for American Progress* (2018), https://www.americanprogressaction.org/issues/ guns-crime/news/2018/10/17/172031/devastating-impact-stand-ground-florida/.

195   Cheng Cheng, Mark Hoekstra, "Does strengthening self-defense law deter crime or escalate violence?" *The Journal of Human Resources* 48 (2013): 821, http://business.baylor.edu/Scott_Cunningham/teaching/cheng-and-hoekstra-2013.pdf.

196   American Bar Association, National Task Force on Stand Your Ground Laws. Preliminary Report and Recommendations, 21-22.

197   Chandler McClellan and Erdal Tekin, "Stand Your Ground Laws, Homicides, and Injuries," *Journal of Human Resources* 52, no. 3 (2017): 621-653.

198   The Coalition to Stop Gun Violence, https://www.csgv.org/believe-absolutely-gun-free-zero-tolerance-totally-safe-schools/.

199   John Lott, "UPDATED: Mass Public Shootings Keep Occurring in Gun-Free Zones: 97.8% of Attacks Since 1950," Crime Prevention Research Center, June 15, 2018.

200   Klarevas, Rampage Nation, 161.

201   FBI, A Study of Active Shooter Incidents in the United States Between 2000 and 2013.

202   GVPedia, *Facts About Firearms Policy Initiative*, March 2021.

203   Gabor, *CARNAGE*, 87.

204   Jan van Dijk, John Kesteren, and Paul Smit, *Criminal Victimization in International Perspective. United Nations Office of Drugs and Crime, 2007*, https://repository.wodc.nl/bitstream/handle/20.500.12832/1204/ob257_full_text_tcm28-69406.pdf?sequence=1.

205   Statistics Canada, "Criminal Victimization: An International Perspective," *Juristat* 22 (2002), https://www150.statcan.gc.ca/n1/en/pub/85-002-x/85-002-x2002004-eng.pdf?st=Br09eXgP.

206   Franklin Zimring and Gordon Hawkins, *Crime Is Not the Problem: Lethal Violence in America* (New York: Oxford University Press, 1999).

207   Zimring and Hawkins, *Crime Is Not the Problem*, 106.

208   Scott Armstrong, "Top Video Game Markets in the World," *Christian Science Monitor*, March 16,2012, https://www.csmonitor.com/USA/Society/2012/0316/Top-video-game-markets-in-the-world/United-Kingdom.

209   Kate Masters, "Media Coverage of the Mentally Ill Exaggerates Their Role in Gun Violence," *The Trace*, June 6,2016, https://www.thetrace.org/2016/06/media-coverage-mentally-ill-exaggerates-role-gun-violence/; swanson pdf.

210   Everytown for Gun Safety, *Analysis of Recent Mass Shootings,2015*.

211   AJ Willingham and Saeed Ahmed, "Mass Shootings in America Are a Serious Problem and These 9 Charts Show Just Why," *CNN.com*, November 26, 2017, https://www.cnn.com/2016/06/13/health/mass-shootings-in-america-in-charts-and-graphs-trnd/index.html.

212   WHO International Consortium in Psychiatric Epidemiology, "Cross-National Comparisons of the Prevalences and Correlates of Mental Disorder," *Bulletin of the World Health Organization* 78 (2000): 413, https://www.ncbi.nlm.nih.gov/pmc/articles/PMC2560724/pdf/10885160.pdf.

213   Gun Violence Archive, *Past Summary Ledgers,* https://www.gunviolencearchive.org/past-tolls.

214   Richard Friedman, "Psychiatrists Can't Stop Mass Killers," *The New York* Times, October 11, 2017, https://www.nytimes.com/2017/10/11/opinion/psychiatrists-mass-killers.html.

215   Benedict Carey, "Are Mass Murderers Insane? Usually Not, Researchers Say," *The New York Times*, November 8, 2017, https://www.nytimes.com/2017/11/08/health/mass-murderers-mental-illness.html.

216   Gabor, *CARNAGE*, 91.

217   Rachel Swaner et al., *"Gotta Make Your Own Heaven': Gun, Safety, and the Edge of Adulthood in New York City* (Center for Court Innovation, 2020).

218   Gabor, *CARNAGE*, 53.

219   Zimring and Hawkins, *Crime is Not the Problem*, 109.

220   *Schenck v. United States*, https://www.oyez.org/cases/1900-1940/249us47.

221   The Articles of Confederation, https://usconstitution.net/articles.html.

222   Michael Waldman, *The Second Amendment: A Biography* (New York: Simon & Schuster, 2014), 27.

223   Michael Waldman, "How the NRA Rewrote the Second Amendment," *Politico Magazine*, May 2014, https://www.politico.com/magazine/story/2014/05/nra-guns-second-amendment-106856/.

224   Joseph Story, *Commentaries on the Constitution of the United States, 1833*, http://resources.utulsa.edu/law/classes/rice/Constitutional/Storey/00_story_vol1_intro.html.

225   Saul Cornell, *A Well Regulated Militia: The Founding Fathers and the Origins of Gun Control in America* (New York: Oxford University Press, 2006).

226   Waldman, "How the NRA Rewrote the Second Amendment."

227   *District of Columbia v. Heller* 554 US 570 (2008), 2.

228   *New York State Pistol Association, Inc. et al. v. Bruen.*

229   John Lowy and Kelly Sampson, "The Right Not to be Shot: Public Safety, Private Guns, and the Constellation of Constitutional Liberties," *Georgetown Journal of Law and Public Policy* 14 (2016): 189.

230   Areto Imoukhuede, "Gun Rights and the New Lochnerism," *Seton Hall Law Review* 47 (2017): 329.

231   United Nations, *Universal Declaration of Human Rights*, https://www.un.org/en/about-us/universal-declaration-of-human-rights.

232   United Nations, *International Covenant on Civil and Political Rights*, https://www.ohchr.org/en/professionalinterest/pages/ccpr.aspx.

233   Amnesty International, *In the Line of Fire: Human Rights and the US Gun Violence Crisis*, 2018, 5, https://www.amnestyusa.org/wp-content/uploads/2018/09/egv_exec_sum.pdf.

234   Thomas Gabor, "The Right of Americans to be Protected From Gun Violence," *Washington University Journal of Law and Policy* 66 (2021): 43.

235   Gabor, "The Right of Americans to be Protected From Gun Violence," 50.

236   *New York v. Quarles* 467 U.S. 649

237   *Hill v. State* 53 Ga. 472 (1874)

238   35 Tex. 473, 478-81 (1872)

239 Everytown for Gun Safety and the Armed Conflict Location & Event Data Project
     (ACLED), *Armed Assembly: Guns, Demonstrations and Political Violence in
     America*, August 23, 2021, https://everytownresearch.org/report/armed-assembly-
     guns-demonstrations-and-political-violence-in-america/#armed-demonstrations-
     in-america.

240 Diana Palmer, *Fired Up or Shut Down: The Chilling Effect of Open Carry on First
     Amendment Expression at Public Protests*, Doctoral dissertation, Northeastern
     University, 2021, https://www.proquest.com/openview/d369586f3e6419d08e021
     6872c60f2a2/1?pq-origsite=gscholar&cbl=18750&diss=y.

241 Maggie Astor, "White Nationalists Want to March Again. Charlottesville Says No,"
     The New York Times, December 12, 2017, https://www.nytimes.com/2017/12/12/
     us/charlottesville-protest-permit-denied.html.

242 Jamie Ducharme, "A Third of Americans Avoid Certain Places Because They
     Fear Mass Shootings," *Time*, August 15, 2019, https://time.com/5653218/mass-
     shootings-stress/.

243 Firmin DeBrabander, "How Guns Could Censor College Classrooms," *The Atlantic*,
     March 2016, https://www.theatlantic.com/education/archive/2016/03/the-steep-
     cost-of-allowing-guns-in-the-college-classroom/472296/.

244 Stephen Curry, "Living, Loving and Dying in Church," *The New York Times*,
     November 7, 2017, https://www.nytimes.com/2017/11/07/opinion/shooting-
     texas-church.html.

245 Gabor, *Confronting Gun Violence in America*, 224.

246 1 Alive Staff, "Music Midtown Cancellation Could Mean $50 Million Loss to
     Economy," *11alive.com,* August 2, 2022, https://www.11alive.com/article/
     entertainment/atlantas-music-midtown-festival-cancellation-50-million-loss-
     economy/85-5fd16421-23e8-43dc-ad8d-cfe8459fa25c.

247 Jennifer Mascia, "Second Amendment Sanctuaries, Explained," *The Trace*, January
     14, 2020, https://www.thetrace.org/2020/01/second-amendment-sanctuary-
     movement/.

248 Mascia, "Second Amendment Sanctuaries, Explained."

249 Jennifer Mascia and Olga Pierce, "Youth Gun Suicide is Rising, Especially
     Among Children of Color," *The Trace*, February 24, 2022, https://www.thetrace.
     org/2022/02/firearm-suicide-rate-cdc-data-teen-mental-health-research/.

250 James Alan Fox, "Gun Control or Carry Permits Won't Stop Mass Murder," *CNN.
     com*, July 21, 2012, https://www.cnn.com/2012/07/20/opinion/fox-mass-murder/
     index.html.

251 Gabor, *Confronting Gun Violence in America*, 8.

252 Grinshteyn and Hemenway, "Violent Death Rates in the US Compared to Those of
     the Other High-Income Countries, 2015."

253 Gun Violence Archive, *Past Summary Ledgers*.

254 Freedom House, *Countries and Territories*, https://freedomhouse.org/countries/
     freedom-world/scores.

255 Mayo Clinic, *Coronary Artery Disease*, https://www.mayoclinic.org/diseases-conditions/coronary-artery-disease/symptoms-causes/syc-20350613.

256 Ronald Clarke, *Situational Crime Prevention, 2nd Ed.* (Guilderland, NY: Harrow and Heston, 1997).

257 Kleck and McElrath, "The Effects of Weaponry on Human Violence."

258 Scott Philips and Michael Maume, "Have Gun Will Shoot: Weapon Instrumentality, Intent, and the Violent Escalation of Conflict," *Homicide Studies* 11, no. 4 (2007): 272.

259 William Wells and Julie Horney, "Weapon Effects and Individual Intent to Do Harm: Influences on the Escalation of Violence," *Criminology* 40, no. 2 (2006): 265.

260 Nicholas Kristof, "How to Win an Argument About Guns," https://nygunforum.com/threads/nyt-how-to-win-an-argument-about-guns.19314/.

261 Gabor, *Confronting Gun Violence in America*, 194-197.

262 Gabor, *Confronting Gun Violence in America*, 197.

263 Linda Saltzman et al., "Weapon Involvement and Injury Outcomes in Family and Intimate Assaults," *Journal of the American Medical Association* 267, no. 22 (1992): 3043, https://pubmed.ncbi.nlm.nih.gov/1588718/; Franklin Zimring, "Is Gun Control Likely to Reduce Violent Killings?" *University of Chicago Law Review* 35, no. 4 (1968): 721.

264 Kay Jamison, *Night Falls Fast: Understanding Suicide* (New York: Knopf, 1999), 47.

265 Jose Bertolote et al., "Deaths from Pesticide Poisoning: A Global Response," *British Journal of Psychiatry* 189, no. 3 (2006): 201.

266 Keith Hawton, "Restriction of Access to Methods of Suicide as a means of suicide prevention. In Keith Hawton (editor), *Prevention and Treatment of Suicidal Behavior: From Science to Practice* (Oxford: Oxford University Press, 2005), 281.

267 National Institute of Justice, *Program profile—police foot patrol—Philadelphia 2009*, https://crimesolutions.ojp.gov/ratedprograms/234.

268 Mark Obbie, "The Wonk's Guide to What Works, and What Doesn't, When Policing Violent Crime," *The Trace*, August 11, 2016, https://www.thetrace.org/2016/08/policing-tactics-what-works/.

269 Marla Becker et al., "Caught in the Crossfire: The Effects of a Peer-Based Intervention Program for Violently Injured Youth," *Journal of Adolescent Health* 34 (2004): 177.

270 Tina Cheng et al., "Effectiveness of a Mentor-Implemented Violence Prevention Intervention for Assault-Injured Youth Presenting to the Emergency Department: Results of a Randomized Trial," *Pediatrics* 122 (2008): 938.

271 M. Burgos, "Deputies Receive More than 1,100 Guns at Gun Swap Event," *ABC Action News*, October 6, 2018, https://www.abcactionnews.com/news/deputies-receive-more-than-1-100-guns-at-gun-swap-event.

272 Rebecca Dyer, "Academe Versus US gun culture." *Inside Higher Ed*, March 29, 2018, https://www.insidehighered. com/views/2018/03/29/growing-movement-divest-gun-manufacturers-opinion.

273   Jon Schuppe, "How a Seattle Nun Led a Shareholder Revolt Against Gun Makers,"
      NBC News, September 30, 2018, https://www.nbcnews.com/news/us-news/how-
      seattle-nun-led-shareholder-revolt-against-gun-makers-n915006.

274   "Reach Beyond Domestic Violence, History." Available at: https://reachma.org/
      who-we-are/history/.

275   Doherty, "A Public Opinion Trend That Matters."

276   Wayne LaPierre, *Guns, Crime, and Freedom* (Washington, DC: Regnery Publishing,
      1994), 171.

277   Karp, *Civilian Firearm Holdings*.

278   Martin Killias and Nora Markwalder, "Firearms and Homicide in Europe," In M. Liem
      and W. Pridemore (eds.). *Handbook of European Homicide Research* (New York:
      Springer, 2012), 264.

279   Amulya Shankar, "In Israel, Gun Ownership is a Privilege Rather Than a Right," *The
      World*, (November 21, 2017), https://theworld.org/stories/2017-11-21/israel-gun-
      ownership-privilege-rather-right.

280   Jon Greenberg, "Fact-Checking Ben Carson's Claim that Gun Control Laws
      Allowed the Nazis to Carry Out Holocaust," *Politifact*, October 26, 2015, https://
      www.politifact.com/factchecks/2015/oct/26/ben-carson/fact-checking-ben-carson-
      nazi-guns/.

281   Stephen Halbrook, "Nazi Firearms Law and the Disarming of the German Jews,"
      Arizona Journal of International and Comparative Law 17, no. 3 (2000), 49.

282   United States Holocaust Memorial Museum, *Germany: Jewish Population in 1933*,
      https://encyclopedia.ushmm.org/content/en/article/germany-jewish-population-
      in-1933.

283   Bernard Harcourt, "On the NRA, Adolph Hitler, Gun Registration and the Nazi Gun
      Laws: Exploding the Cultural Wars," Public Law Working Paper No. 67 (Chicago:
      University of Chicago, 2004).

284   Gabor, *Confronting Gun Violence in America*, 197-201.

285   Garen Wintemute, "Firearm Retailers' Willingness to Participate in an Illegal
      Purchase," *Journal of Urban Health* 87, no. 5 (2010): 865, https://www.ncbi.nlm.nih.
      gov/pmc/articles/PMC2937134/.

286   Office of the Inspector General, *Inspections of Firearm Dealers by the Bureau of
      Alcohol, Tobacco, Firearms, and Explosives* (Washington, DC: US Department of
      Justice, 2004), iii.

287   Henigan, Lethal Logic, 152.

288   Gabor, *Confronting Gun Violence in America*, 124-125.

289   Giffords Law Center, *Annual Gun Law Scorecard*, https://giffords.org/lawcenter/
      resources/scorecard/.

290   John Gramlich and Drew Desilver, "Despite Recent Violence, Chicago Is Far
      from the US "Murder Capital," *Pew Research Center*, November 13, 2018, http://
      www.pewresearch.org/fact-tank/2014/07/14/despite-recent-shootings-chicago-
      nowhere-near-u-s-murder-capital/.

291 Shelby Bremer, "The Majority of Guns Used in Chicago Crimes Come from Outside Illinois: Report," *NBC Chicago*, October 29, 2017, https://www.nbcchicago.com/news/national-international/chicago-gun-trace-report-2017/27140/.

292 Luntz Global, Gun Owners Poll, July 24, 2012.

293 Alicia Samuels, "Gun Owners and Non-Gun Owners Agree on Many Gun Safety Proposals," *Johns Hopkins University Hub*, May 17, 2018, https://hub.jhu.edu/2018/05/17/gun-control-measures-gun-owners-survey/.

294 Cook and Goss, *The Gun Debate*, 55.

295 Patricia Tjaden and Nancy Thoennes, *Extent, Nature, and Consequences of Intimate Partner Violence. Findings from the National Violence Against Women Survey* (Washington, DC: Office of Justice Programs, 2000).

296 Anthony Braga and David Weisburd, "The Effects of Focused-Deterrence Strategies on Crime," *Journal of Research in Crime and Delinquency* 49, no. 3 (2012): 323.

297 National Institute of Justice, *Five Things About Deterrence*, May 2016, https://www.ojp.gov/pdffiles1/nij/247350.pdf.

298 Thomas Gabor, *Everybody Does It: Crime by the Public* (Toronto: University of Toronto Press, 1994).

299 Everytown for Gun Safety, *Mass Shootings*, https://www.everytown.org/issues/mass-shootings/.

300 Gary Nunn, "Darwin Shooting: Why Mass Shooting Feels Unfamiliar to Australia," *BBC News*, June 5, 2019, https://www.bbc.com/news/world-australia-48522788.

301 Adam Winkler, "Gun Control is Racist?: The NRA Would Know," *The New Republic*, February 4, 2013, https://newrepublic.com/article/112322/gun-control-racist.

302 Giffords Law Center, *"Stand Your Ground" Laws*, http://lawcenter.giffords.org/gun-laws/policy-areas/guns-in-public/stand-your-ground-laws/.

303 Irina Ivanova, "Number of Guns Made in the US Nearly Tripled Since 2000," *CBS News*, May 18, 2022, https://www.cbsnews.com/news/guns-us-manufacturing-nearly-tripled-since-2000/.

304 U.S. Department of the Treasury, Bureau of Alcohol, Tobacco and Firearms, *Firearms Commerce in the United States 2001/2002*, April 2002, E1-E3.

305 Sophia Ignatidou, "EU-US Cooperation in Tackling Disinformation," *Chatham House*, October 3, 2019, https://www.chathamhouse.org/2019/10/eu-us-cooperation-tackling-disinformation-0/3-countermeasures-disinformation.

306 Craig Anderson, Mark Lepper, and Lee Ross, "Perseverance of Social Theories: The Role of Explanation in the Persistence of Discredited Information," *Journal of Personality and Social Psychology 39, no. 6 (1980):* 1037.

307 Katherine Ognyanova et al., "Misinformation in Action: Fake News Exposure is Linked to Lower Trust in Media, Higher Trust in Government When Your Side is in Power," *The Harvard Kennedy School Misinformation Review*, June 2, 2020, https://misinforeview.hks.harvard.edu/article/misinformation-in-action-fake-news-

exposure-is-linked-to-lower-trust-in-media-higher-trust-in-government-when-your-side-is-in-power/.

308   Zara Abrams, "Controlling the Spread of Misinformation," *American Psychological Association*, March 1, 2021, https://www.apa.org/monitor/2021/03/controlling-misinformation.

309   Joan Biskupic, "Guns: A Second (Amendment) Look," *Washington Post*, May 10, 1995, https://www.washingtonpost.com/wp-srv/national/longterm/supcourt/stories/courtguns051095.htm?noredirect=on.

310   Waldmann, "How the NRA Rewrote the Second Amendment."

311   US Department of Transportation, *Effectiveness of safety and public service messages on dynamic message signs. 2014*, https://ops.fhwa.dot.gov/publications/fhwahop14015/fhwahop14015.pdf.

312   William Jenaway et al., *Determining the Relative Impact of PSAs and Brochures upon General Public Drivers Interfacing With Emergency Service Vehicles* (US Department of Justice, 2012), https://www.ojp.gov/pdffiles1/nij/grants/238779.pdf.

313   PSA Research Center, "Are Public Service Ads Effective?" December 29, 2019, https://www.psaresearch.com/are-public-service-ads-effective/.

314   Rand, *Gun Policy Research Review*, https://www.rand.org/research/gun-policy/analysis.html.

315   William McGuire, "The Effectiveness of Supportive and Refutational Defenses in Immunizing and Restoring Beliefs Against Persuasion," *Sociometry* 24 (1961): 184.

316   Josh Compton, "Inoculation theory," in *The SAGE Handbook of Persuasion: Developments in Theory and Practice, 2nd Edn.*, eds J. Dillard and L. Shen (Thousand Oaks, CA: Sage; 2013), 220–236.

317   John Banas and Stephen Rains, "A Meta-Analysis of Research on Inoculation Theory," *Communication Monographs* 77, no. 3 (2010): 281.

318   Bad News, https://www.getbadnews.com/#play.

319   Gordon Pennycook et al., "Fighting COVID-19 Misinformation on Social Media: Experimental Evidence for a Scalable Accuracy-Nudge Intervention," *Psychological Science* 31, no. 7 (2020): 770, https://journals.sagepub.com/doi/pdf/10.1177/0956797620939054.

320   Rolf Reber and Norbert Schwarz, "Effects of Perceptual Fluency on Judgments of Truth. *Consciousness and Cognition* 8, no. 3 (1999): 338, https://www.sciencedirect.com/science/article/abs/pii/S1053810099903860.

321   Gautam Shahi and Durgesh Nandini, Fake Covid: A Multilingual Cross-Domain Fact Check News Dataset for Covid-19," *Association for the Advancement of Artificial Intelligence*, 2020, https://arxiv.org/ftp/arxiv/papers/2006/2006.11343.pdf.

322   World Health Organization, *Infodemic*, https://www.who.int/health-topics/infodemic#tab=tab_1.

323   K. Graydon et al., "Countering Misinformation: A Multidisciplinary Approach,"
      Big Data and Society (2021), January-June: 1, https://journals.sagepub.com/doi/
      pdf/10.1177/20539517211013848.

324   Graydon et al., "Countering Misinformation."

325   Abrams, "Controlling the Spread of Misinformation."

326   Bence Bago, David Rand, and Gordon Pennycook, "Fake News, Fast and Slow:
      Deliberation Reduces Belief in False (But Not True) News Headlines," *Journal
      of Experimental Psychology 149, no. 8 (2020):* 1608, https://doi.apa.org/
      doiLanding?doi=10.1037%2Fxge0000729.

327   *District of Columbia v. Heller* 554 U.S. 570 (2008).

ABOUT THE AUTHORS

Thomas (Tom) Gabor received his PhD at Ohio State University and has been a professor, researcher, and consultant in the area of gun violence for over thirty-five years. A criminologist and sociologist, Tom was an adviser to the United Nations in its study of international firearms regulation in 1998. He was retained as an expert by the families of the young victims of a mass shooting at Dunblane Primary School in Scotland in 1996. Tom submitted expert testimony to Lord Cullen's Public Inquiry into the massacre, an Inquiry which led to major changes in the United Kingdom's firearms laws. He has also advised numerous government agencies, such as Canada's Department of Justice, Public Safety Canada, Canada's Border Services Agency, and Canada's National Crime Prevention Council.

Tom's recent books include *Confronting Gun Violence in America* (2016), *ENOUGH: Solving America's Gun Violence Crisis* (2019), *and CARNAGE: Preventing Mass Shootings in America* (2020). He has been a contributing writer to *Fortune* magazine and is a regular opinion writer for a number of newspapers. He has also drafted a *Declaration of the Right to Live Free from Gun Violence*, which affirms the right of Americans to be protected from gun violence by their government, based on America's founding documents and on international agreements signed or ratified by the US (see Appendix A).

Tom has appeared on a variety of media programs and has spoken in front of numerous groups concerned about gun violence, including the League of Women Voters, Moms Demand Action for Gun Sense in America,

Indivisibles, March for Our Lives, Brady United Against Gun Violence, and the National Council of Jewish Women, as well as numerous faith groups and community organizations. For more information on his professional activities, please visit: thomasgaborbooks.com

Fred Guttenberg's involvement in gun violence prevention is the result of tragedy. On February 14, 2018, he sent his two children to school at Marjory Stoneman Douglas High School in Parkland, Florida. His daughter Jaime was murdered that day by a teenager with an AR-15, and his son Jesse heard the shots that killed his sister. Only four months prior, Fred's brother Michael died of cancer related to his service at the World Trade Center on 9/11.

Following Fred's involvement in two distinctly American tragedies, he has traveled the country talking about both events but also about perspective, perseverance, and resilience. Since his daughter's murder, Fred has also spent his time traveling the country to confront the issues around gun violence and the legislators who should be doing more to solve it. Fred's mission ultimately led him to write his book *Find the Helpers* (2020). He has been a regular on TV news programs and myriad online and print media. This is now his full-time mission.

Prior to these events, Fred Guttenberg's professional life included over a decade of experience in sales and management with Johnson and Johnson, followed by almost fifteen years as an entrepreneur, building a business that consisted of nineteen Dunkin Donuts eateries, which he sold in November, 2016.

Mango Publishing, established in 2014, publishes an eclectic list of books by diverse authors—both new and established voices—on topics ranging from business, personal growth, women's empowerment, LGBTQ+ studies, health, and spirituality to history, popular culture, time management, decluttering, lifestyle, mental wellness, aging, and sustainable living. We were recently named 2019 *and* 2020's #1 fastest-growing independent publisher by *Publishers Weekly*. Our success is driven by our main goal, which is to publish high-quality books that will entertain readers as well as make a positive difference in their lives.

Our readers are our most important resource; we value your input, suggestions, and ideas. We'd love to hear from you—after all, we are publishing books for you!

Please stay in touch with us and follow us at:

Facebook: Mango Publishing
Twitter: @MangoPublishing
Instagram: @MangoPublishing
LinkedIn: Mango Publishing
Pinterest: Mango Publishing
Newsletter: mangopublishinggroup.com/newsletter

Join us on Mango's journey to reinvent publishing, one book at a time.